JAPAN DATA PROTECTION LAW
A Practical Guide In Comparison With GDPR

Toshio Asai

Copyright © 2018 Toshio Asai

All Rights Reserved.

Introduction

With the development of information technology, the collection and the use of personally identifiable information ("personal information") or personal data (with personal information, collectively referred to as "personal data" unless otherwise noted) by companies have rapidly become on a large scale, and the disclosure of personal data by individuals has become extremely easy by using SNS (social networking services) or other information technologies. In proportion to this, large-scale leakage or other privacy-related problems have become global issues.

Further, as IoT (Internet of Things) will be used anywhere around individuals, it is expected the collection, processing, and use of personal data will increase explosively, and the technology (including artificial intelligence) and business using personal data as "big data" will develop and expand greatly.

With these situations as the background, in Japan, the Act on the Protection of Personal Information ("APPI") was amended and fully enforced from May 30, 2017. One of the reasons is that the General Data Protection Regulation (GDPR) of EU, which strengthens the protection of personal data more than ever, was established, and will be enforced on May 25, 2018.

This book outlines APPI in comparison with and according to the order of the provisions of GDPR. I hope this book will help those interested in APPI understand it.

Toshio Asai
May 2018

Feedback. Comments on this book (suggestions for improvement, error reports, etc.) from readers are welcome. If you have any comments, please send them to:

review@theunilaw.com

Acronyms, Abbreviations, Key Terms and Relevant URLs   (in alphabetic order)

- **API (Anonymously Processed Information)**
  The information produced by processing personal information so that a specific individual cannot be identified
- **API GL**
  The "Guidelines of the Act on the Protection of Personal Information (Anonymously Processed Information)" published by PPC
  (In Japanese language only)
  https://www.ppc.go.jp/files/pdf/guidelines04.pdf
- **API Report**
  The "Report by the Personal Information Protection Commission Secretariat: Anonymously Processed Information - Towards Balanced Promotion of Personal Data Utilization and Consumer Trust" published by PPC
  (A version with English translation)
  https://www.ppc.go.jp/files/pdf/The_PPC_Secretariat_Report_on_Anonymously_Processed_Information.pdf
- **APPI**
  The "Act on the Protection of Personal Information" (English translations)
  https://www.ppc.go.jp/files/pdf/Act_on_the_Protection_of_Personal_Information.pdf
  http://www.japaneselawtranslation.go.jp/law/detail/?x=55&y=16&re=01&co=1&ia=03&yo=&gn=&sy=&ht=&no=&bu=&ta=&ky=%E5%80%8B%E4%BA%BA%E6%83%85%E5%A0%B1%E3%81%AE%E4%BF%9D%E8%AD%B7%E3%81%AB%E9%96%A2%E3%81%99%E3%82%8B&page=20
- **Business operator**
  The business operator handling personal information, to which APPI applies.
- **Confirmation and Record GL**
  The "Guidelines on the Act on the Protection of Personal Information (Confirmation and Record at the Time of Provision of Personal Data to a Third Party)" published by PPC

(In Japanese language only)
https://www.ppc.go.jp/files/pdf/guidelines03.pdf
- **Data exporter**
The business operator which provides personal data to a third party in a foreign country
- **Data importer**
The third party in a foreign country which receives personal data from a business operator
- **Foreign GL**
The "Guidelines on the Act on the Protection of Personal Information (Provision of Personal Data to a Third Party in a Foreign Country)" published by PPC
(In Japanese language only)
https://www.ppc.go.jp/files/pdf/guidelines02.pdf
- **GDPR**
The General Data Protection Regulation of EU
http://eur-lex.europa.eu/legal-content/EN/TXT/?uri=uriserv:OJ.L_.2016.119.01.0001.01.ENG&toc=OJ:L:2016:119:TOC
- **General exceptional cases**
  (a) When the handling (of personal data) is required or authorized under laws or regulations;
  (b) When the handling is necessary to protect the data subject's life, body or property and it is difficult to obtain his or her consent;
  (c) When the handling is particularly necessary for the improvement of public health or the promotion of healthy development of children and it is difficult to obtain the data subject's consent; or
  (d) When the handling is necessary to cooperate with a central government organization or a local government, or a person entrusted by them in their executing their legal duties and obtaining the data subject's consent is likely to impede the execution of such duties.
- **General GL**
The "Guidelines on the Act on the Protection of Personal Information" published by PPC
(In Japanese language only)
https://www.ppc.go.jp/files/pdf/guidelines01.pdf

- **Individual identification codes**
  The codes prescribed by the Order as those that can identify a specific individual.
  As of May 2018, those prescribed by the Order include DNA sequences, facial appearances, iris patterns, vocalizations, postures and walking movements, hand or finger vein patterns, fingerprints or palm prints, passport numbers, driver's license numbers, resident register codes, the Individual Numbers, residence card numbers, and certain identifiers relating to pension, health insurance, nursing care insurance, and employment insurance (Order 1, Rules 2,3,4).
- **Individual Number**
  A 12-digit number assigned to every Japanese citizen or every resident of Japan falling under certain conditions under the Number Act
- **Measures in Case of Data Leakage**
  The "Measures to Be Taken in the Event of Leakage of Personal Data" published by PPC
  (In Japanese language only)
  https://www.ppc.go.jp/files/pdf/iinkaikokuzi01.pdf
- **Number Act**
  The "Act on the Use of Numbers to Identify a Specific Individual in Administrative Procedures"
  (English translation)
  https://www.ppc.go.jp/files/pdf/en3.pdf
- **Opt-out mechanism**
  The following mechanism:
  The business operator may provide personal data (excluding personal information requiring special consideration) to a third party (in Japan) without obtaining the data subject's prior consent when both of the following conditions are satisfied in accordance with the Rules (APPI 23(2)).
  (a) Before the provision to the third party, the business operator shall notify the data subjects of certain items concerning the provision or make them easily accessible to the data subjects, and report the items to PPC; and

(b) The business operator shall discontinue the provision to the third party upon request from the data subject.
- **Order**
  The Cabinet order to enforce APPI
  (English Translation)
  https://www.ppc.go.jp/files/pdf/Cabinet_Order.pdf
- **Personal data**
  The personal information constituting a personal information database etc (APPI 2(6))
- **Personal information**
  (a) The information which can identify a specific individual, including information which can be readily collated with other information and thereby identify a specific individual, or
  (b) The information that contains the individual identification codes (APPI 2(1))
- **Personal information database etc.**
  The collection of information:
  (a) which is systematically organized so that specific personal information can be searched using a computer; or
  (b) which is designated by the Order as being systematically organized so that specific personal information can be easily searched (APPI 2(4)).
- **Personal information requiring special consideration**
  The personal information which contains data subject's race, creed or beliefs, social status, medical record, criminal record or the fact that he or she was a victim or suspect or defendant of a crime, certain physical or mental handicaps, or other descriptions designated by the Order as those of which the handling requires special consideration to prevent discrimination, prejudice, or other unfair disadvantages (APPI 2(3), Order 2, Rule 5).
- **PPC**
  The Personal Information Protection Commission, Japan (PPC's English Website)
  https://www.ppc.go.jp/en/
- **Public Institutions**

A central government organization, local government, or independent administrative agencies
- **Q&A**
  The "Q&A on the Guidelines on the Act on the Protection of Personal Information and the Measures to Be Taken in the Event of Leakage of Personal Data" published by PPC
  (In Japanese language only)
  https://www.ppc.go.jp/files/pdf/kojouhouQA.pdf
- **Retained Personal Data**
  The personal data which the business operator has the authority to disclose, correct, add other content to or delete, discontinue using or delete, and discontinue providing to a third party, excluding the personal data which are deleted within six (6) months from the collection thereof (APPI 2(7)).
- **Rules**
  The PPC rules to enforce APPI
  (English Translation)
  https://www.ppc.go.jp/files/pdf/PPC_rules.pdf
- **Specific Personal Information**
  The information containing the Individual Numbers

Table of Contents

Introduction..3
Acronyms, Abbreviations, Key Terms and Relevant URLs...5
I. Background of the Enactment of APPI in 2003..........15
II. Background of 2017 Amendment...............................15
III. Subject-Matter and Objectives of APPI......................17
IV. English Translation of APPI, and the Guidelines on APPI.. 17
V. Definitions of Basic Concepts..................................19
   1. Personal Information..19
   2. Personal Data..20
   3. Retained Personal Data...21
   4. Personal Information Requiring Special Consideration 22
   5. Business Operator Handling Personal Information. 22
   6. Handling etc. of Personal Data..............................23
VI. General Exceptions to the Application.....................23
   1. Public Institutions...24
   2. News Media etc... 24
   3. Individual Numbers...25
VII. Extraterritorial Application....................................... 25
   1. Collection in Relation to the Offering of Goods or Services...25
   2. Application to the Monitoring of Data Subjects.......26
VIII. Principles Relating to Handling of Personal Data....... 26
   1. Restriction of Collection...26
   2. Prohibition of Collecting Personal Information Requiring Special Consideration..........................26
   3. Specification and Restriction of Purpose of Use (Purpose Limitation) 28
   4. Accuracy and the Deletion of Unnecessary Personal Data..29
   5. Obligations in Relation to Providing or Receiving Personal Data...29
     (1). The Principle of the Data Subject's Consent...29
     (2). Provision to a Third Party Using Opt-out Mechanism...30
     (3). Exceptions in the Cases of Entrustment of Handling, Merger, Joint-Use, Etc..................32

	(4). Record Obligations Concerning Providing or Receiving Personal Data...........................33
	(5). Use of Cloud Services..............................36
	6. Difference from GDPR................................38
IX.	Transparency: Information Disclosure to the Data Subject...39
	1. Business Operator's Obligations......................40
	(1). Disclosure Concerning the Collection of Personal Data and the Change of the Purpose of Use...40
	(2). Disclosure Concerning Retained Personal Data...41
	2. Difference from GDPR................................. 42
X.	Rights of the Data Subject...................................42
	1. Right to Request Disclosure (Right of Access) 43
	2. Right to Request Correction...............................43
	3. Right to Request Discontinuance of the Use or the Provision to a Third Party................................43
	4. Difference from GDPR................................. 43
	5. The Nature of the Data Subject's Rights...............44
	6. Right to Be Forgotten....................................45
	(1). Background..45
	(2). Summary of the Supreme Court Decision.......45
	(3). The Legal Basis of the Right to Be Forgotten...46
XI.	Measures and Certification of Compliance................46
XII.	No Requirement to Designate a Representative in Japan..47
XIII.	Entrustment of the Handling of Personal Data to a Third Party... 47
XIV.	The Obligation to Record the Handling of Personal Data..47
XV.	Security of Handling...48
	1. Basic Principles... 48
	2. Supervision of Employees or a Third Party............48
	3. A Summary of PPC's Recommendations on Security Measures...48
	4. Difference from GDPR................................. 49
XVI.	Notification of Data Leakage Etc. to the Supervisory Authority and Data Subjects................................... 50
XVII.	No Requirement for Data Protection Impact Assessment (DPIA)...52

XVIII. No Requirement to Designate a Data Protection Officer (DPO)..................52
XIX. Codes of Conduct and Certification Mechanism.........53
  1. Codes of Conduct... 53
  2. Certification Mechanism..................................53
    (1). The Outline of Privacy Mark System in Japan. 54
    (2). APEC CBPR (Cross-Border Privacy Rules) ... 54
XX. Provision of Personal Data to a Third Party in a Foreign Country..................56
  1. The Principle of the Data Subject's Consent..........56
  2. The Exception under a Contract or Internal Rules or an International Framework................57
  3. Use of a Foreign Company's Cloud Service..........57
  4. Difference from GDPR..................................... 59
  5. Japan EU Negotiation Toward Mutual Adequacy Findings....................... 62
XXI. Supervisory Authority..62
XXII. Remedies, Liability, and Penalties........................63
  1. Relevant Provisions of APPI...............................63
  2. Difference from GDPR..................................... 64
XXIII.   Anonymously Processed Information................. 64
  1. Definition..64
  2. Background and Objectives...............................64
  3. Business Operator's Obligations.........................65
    (1). Obligations of the Producer of Anonymously Processed Information............................... 65
    (2). Obligations of the Business Operator Other Than the Producer.......................................67
    (3). Obligations Not Imposed Concerning Anonymously Processed Information..............67
  4. Guidelines on Anonymously Processed Information.. 68
  5. Comparison with "Pseudonymization" in GDPR......68
    (1). "Anonymously Processed Information" in APPI...68
    (2). "Statistical Information" in APPI.....................70
XXIV.   Protection of Individual Numbers...................... 70
  1. An Overview..70
  2. Restriction of Collection....................................71
  3. Restriction of Use 72
  4. Restriction of Provision to a Third Party................73

    5. Security of Handling... 73
XXV. Restriction of Advertisements by E-mails................74
XXVI. Regulations on Cookies......................................75
XXVII.   Sample Agreements for the Provision of Personal
    Data to a Third Party in a Foreign Country.................75
    1. PERSONAL DATA PROVISION AGREEMENT.... 77
    2. AGREEMENT FOR ENTRUSTMENT OF HANDLING
        OF PERSONAL DATA......................................98
Index...113
About the Author...115
Authors' Articles and Books..117

I. Background of the Enactment of APPI in 2003

With the publication of OECD guidelines in 1980 and the enactment of EU Data Protection Directive in 1995 as the background, the Cabinet of Japan established a working group to study the protection of personal information in 1999, and, as a result of it, the "Act on the Protection of Personal Information" ("APPI") was enacted in 2003 and fully enforced in 2005.

APPI establishes a basic framework of the handling of personal information for the public and private sectors and the specific rules for private entities to handle personal information. With respect to the specific rules for the public sector, the "Act on the Protection of Personal Information Held by Administrative Organs[1]" and the "Act on the Protection of Personal Information Held by Independent Administrative Agencies, etc.[2]" were enacted.

This book explains the obligations under APPI of business operators in the private sector who handle personal information (the "business operator").

II. Background of 2017 Amendment

---

[1] Act on the Protection of Personal Information Held by Administrative Organs
(English translation)
http://www.japaneselawtranslation.go.jp/law/detail/?x=0&y=0&re=01&co=1&ia=03&yo=&gn=&sy=&ht=&no=&bu=&ta=&ky=%E5%80%8B%E4%BA%BA%E6%83%85%E5%A0%B1&page=12

[2] Act on the Protection of Personal Information Held by Independent Administrative Agencies, etc.
(in Japanese language only)
http://elaws.e-gov.go.jp/search/elawsSearch/elaws_search/lsg0500/detail?lawId=415AC0000000059

The amendment to APPI that came into effect in May 2017 was made based on the recognition that the establishment of the environment to utilize personal data while considering the privacy protection had become an urgent task in light of the following:

(a) The ways of use of personal data which were not anticipated at the time of the enactment of APPI in 2003 have become possible because of the development of information and communication technologies. As a result, the gray area of the law in which it is difficult to determine whether certain data fall under the personal information or not has expanded;

(b) It became necessary to establish an environment which ensures proper utilization of big data containing personal data; and

(c) Business activities have become global, and a lot of data have been distributed beyond the borders.

With respect to (a) and (b) above, the following cases had been kept in mind.

In June 2013, East Japan Railway Company received criticism by the public in respect of privacy about the fact that it had provided to other companies the record of passengers' getting on and off, although specific individuals could not be identified by the record.

In November of the same year, NTT DoCoMo, a mobile telecommunications carrier, also received criticism by the public in respect of privacy about the fact that it had provided to other companies the GPS location data of NTT DoCoMo users, although specific individuals could not be identified by the data because the raw data had been statistically processed.

The Japanese government considered (i) one of the causes of such social phenomenon (i.e. criticism by the public) was that APPI was partly unclear on the rules of the usage of personal data, (ii) but it was necessary to promote proper utilization of personal data while protecting data privacy, and therefore, (iii) it was necessary to clarify the rules.

As a result, under the amended APPI enforced in May 2017, the definition of personal information was revised to be more specific, and provisions were added concerning "anonymously processed information" (the information produced by processing personal information so that a specific individual cannot be identified) to utilize big data.

Regarding (c) above, provisions were added in the amended APPI with respect to the provision of personal data to a third party in a foreign country, referencing the restriction under GDPR of the transfer of personal data outside the European Economic Area (EEA).

III. Subject-Matter and Objectives of APPI

APPI states that "This Act aims to protect an individual's rights and interests while considering the utility of personal information, including that the proper and effective utilization of personal information contributes to the creation of new industries and the realization of a vibrant economic society and the enriched quality of life for the people" (1) (figures are the numbers of the articles of APPI or other laws, the same in this book). The utilization of personal data is more emphasized when compared with GDPR.

IV. English Translation of APPI, and the Guidelines on APPI

On the website[3] of the Personal Information Protection Commission, Japan ("PPC"), the national supervisory authority of APPI, the English translations of APPI and the

---

[3] The website of Personal Information Protection Commission, Japan ("PPC")
https://www.ppc.go.jp/en/

Cabinet order (the "Order") and the PPC rules (the "Rules") to enforce APPI are posted.

The website is also posting the following guidelines, Q&A and a report prepared and published by PPC (they are in Japanese language only except otherwise noted below). These are not legally binding, but the interpretation and action guidelines on APPI that PPC expects business operators to follow.

- Guidelines on the Act on the Protection of Personal Information (General Rules) (the "**General GL**")
- Guidelines on the Act on the Protection of Personal Information (Provision of Personal Data to a Third Party in a Foreign Country) ("**Foreign GL**")
- Guidelines on the Act on the Protection of Personal Information (Confirmation and Record at the Time of Provision of Personal Data to a Third Party) ("**Confirmation and Record GL**")
- Guidelines of the Act on the Protection of Personal Information (Anonymously Processed Information) ("**API GL**")
- Report by the Personal Information Protection Commission Secretariat: Anonymously Processed Information - Towards Balanced Promotion of Personal Data Utilization and Consumer Trust (there is a version with English translation) ("**API Report**")
- Measures to Be Taken in the Event of Leakage of Personal Data ("**Measures in the Case of Data Leakage**")
- Q&A on the Guidelines on the Act on the Protection of Personal Information and the Measures to Be Taken in the Event of Leakage of Personal Data ("**Q&A**")
- Points of Consideration in Handling Health-Related Personal Information in the Employment Management
- Various guidelines in the financial sector
- Various guidelines in the medical field
- Various guidelines in other sectors or fields (telecommunications business, broadcasting, postal business, letter delivery business, genetic information)

V. Definitions of Basic Concepts

1. Personal Information

APPI defines the "personal information" as the information about a living individual that falls under any of the following (2(1)):
(a) the information which can identify a specific individual (the "data subject") by a name, date of birth, or other descriptions contained in the information, including information which can be readily collated with other information and thereby identify a specific individual; or
(b) the information that contains the "individual identification codes."

The "individual identification codes" (or personal identification codes) are characters, numbers, symbols, and/or other codes which are prescribed by the Order as those that can identify a specific individual (2(2)). As of May 2018, those prescribed by the Order include DNA sequences, facial appearances, iris patterns, vocalizations, postures and walking movements, hand or finger vein patterns, fingerprints or palm prints, passport numbers, driver's license numbers, resident register codes, the Individual Numbers (explained in VI-3 and XXIV), residence card numbers, and certain identifiers relating to pension, health insurance, nursing care insurance, and employment insurance (Order 1, Rules 2,3,4).

Most of the personal information defined in APPI would also fall under the personal data defined in GDPR (4(1)). In GDPR, location data and online identifiers are specifically listed. However, as they must relate to a natural person who can be identified by reference to them, they are also the personal information defined in APPI. Therefore, there would be no substantial difference between the scope of the personal information defined in APPI and the personal data defined in GDPR, at least theoretically.

The personal information defined in APPI includes not only personal data (explained in 2 below) but also the

19

personal information which is not personal data (e.g. personal information which is written on paper and not systematically structured).   All the provisions in APPI concerning the obligations of the business operator apply to personal data, while only the following provisions apply to the personal information which is not personal data.

<Provisions Which Apply to the Personal Information That Is Not Personal Data>
(a) Article 15: Specification of the purposes of use
(b) Article 16: Restriction concerning the purpose of use
(c) Article 17: Proper collection
(d) Article 18: Notification of the purpose of use at the time of collection
(e) Article 35: Proper handling of the data subjects' complaints

2. Personal Data

The "personal data" is defined in APPI as the personal information constituting a personal information database etc. (2(6)). The "personal information database etc." means the collection of information which has been systematically organized so that specific personal information can be searched using a computer (2(4)(i)).

In addition, even when a computer is not used, if a collection of personal information written on paper is arranged and classified according to certain rules (e.g. alphabetical order) and a table of contents, index, etc. are attached to it, and thereby specific personal information can be easily searched, the collection falls under the "personal information database etc." (2(4)(ii) [e.g. indexed staff registration cards of a temporary staffing agency: General GL p.17]

GDPR "applies to the processing of personal data wholly or partly by automated means and to the processing other than by automated means of personal data which form part of a filing system or are intended to form part of a filing system." (2(1)).   The "personal information database etc." would correspond to the "filing system" in GDPR, as the latter is defined as any structured set of personal data which are accessible according to specific criteria (4(6)).

3. Retained Personal Data

In APPI, the "retained personal data" is defined as the personal data which the business operator has the authority to disclose, correct, add other content to or delete, discontinue using or delete, and discontinue providing to a third party. However, it excludes the personal data which are deleted within six (6) months from the collection thereof (2(7), Q&A p.12). In GDPR, there is neither a term that corresponds to retained personal data nor such exclusion. However, the business operator who owns the retained personal data would correspond to the "controller" in GDPR, as the latter is defined as the natural or legal person, public authority, agency or any other body which "determines the purposes and means of the processing of personal data."

The following provisions in APPI apply only to the business operator who owns retained personal information:

(a) **Article 27:** Public disclosure etc. concerning retained personal data
(b) **Article 28:** Disclosure of retained personal data at the request of the data subject
(c) **Article 29:** Correction, addition, or deletion of retained personal data at the request of the data subject
(d) **Article 30:** Discontinuance of the use of or deletion or the discontinuance of the provision to a third party of retained personal data at the request of the data subject
(e) **Articles 31-33:** Procedural provisions concerning Articles 27 through 30
(f) **Article 23 (2):** Discontinuance of the provision to a third party of personal data on which the business operator uses the opt-out mechanism (explained in VIII-5) at the request of the data subject. Although Article 23 (2) stipulates about the "personal data," it substantially relates only to the retained personal data of the business operator.

The relationship between personal information, personal data, and retained personal data could be represented as follows:

Personal information>Personal data>Retained Personal Data

4. Personal Information Requiring Special Consideration

APPI defines the "personal information requiring special consideration" as the personal information which contains the data subject's race, creed or beliefs, social status (*), medical record, criminal record or the fact that he or she was a victim or suspect or defendant of a crime, certain physical or mental handicaps, or other descriptions designated by the Order as those of which the handling requires special consideration to prevent discrimination, prejudice, or other unfair disadvantages (2(3), Order 2, Rule 5). [(*) typically, being the people who have been historically discriminated against, but not including mere occupational position or educational background: General GL p.12]

As of May 2018, the Order does not designate the trade-union membership and information concerning sex life or sexual orientation as the above-mentioned descriptions. It may be said that the scope of the "personal information requiring special consideration" is narrower than that of the "special categories of personal data" defined in GDPR, as the latter includes the trade-union membership and data concerning sex life or sexual orientation (9).

5. Business Operator Handling Personal Information

APPI applies to a "business operator handling personal information." It means the natural or legal person or any other body which handles a personal information database etc. for use in business (for profit or non-profit). However, it does not include a central government organization, local government, or independent administrative agencies (the "Public institutions"). In this book, it is simply referred to as a "business operator."

Before the amendment, APPI also excluded from its application a business operator (usually a small-sized one) if the total number of the individuals identified by the personal data the business operator handles has not exceeded 5,000 at any time during the past six months. This exclusion was abolished by the amendment.

The "processor" in GDPR (2(8)) would correspond to the business operator to whom another business operator entrusts the handling of personal data (APPI 22), and the "controller" in GDPR (2(7)) would correspond to the business operator other than the processor or the business operator who owns the retained personal data as mentioned above.

6. Handling etc. of Personal Data

The terms "handling," "collection," "use," "deletion," and "provision" (of personal data) used in APPI would correspond to the "processing" defined in GDPR. The term "processing" in GDPR, however, is very broad, as it is defined as "any operation or set of operations which is performed on personal data or on sets of personal data, whether or not by automated means, such as <u>collection, recording, organization, structuring, storage, adaptation or alteration, retrieval, consultation, use, disclosure by transmission, dissemination or otherwise making available, alignment or combination, restriction, erasure or destruction</u>"(4(2)). It is unknown whether the "handling" or all the above-mentioned terms used in APPI together cover all the operations included in the "processing" in GDPR.

VI. General Exceptions to the Application

In principle, APPI applies to any natural or legal person or other body which handles any personal information. However, there are the following exceptions.

1. **Public Institutions**

   As already mentioned, APPI establishes a basic framework of the handling of personal information for both the public and private sectors and the specific rules for the private entities to handle personal information. However, with respect to the specific rules for the public sector, the "Act on the Protection of Personal Information Held by Administrative Organs" or the "Act on the Protection of Personal Information Held by Independent Administrative Agencies, etc." applies.

2. **News Media etc.**

   The provisions of APPI on the obligations of the business operator do not apply to the news media, writers, academic organizations, religious organizations, or political organizations, etc. to the extent that they handle personal information for the news report, writing, academic studies, religious activities or political activities, etc. respectively (76(1)). For example, when a newspaper discloses the name of a person in the article regarding a crime committed by him or her, the obligations of the business operator stipulated in APPI are not imposed.
   However, they shall take appropriate measures to ensure the security of personal information and deal with complaints from data subjects about their handling of personal information and shall endeavor to publish such measures (76(2)).

3. **Individual Numbers**

   With respect to the "Individual Number" (a 12-digit number assigned to every Japanese citizen or every resident of Japan falling under certain conditions) and the information containing the Individual Number ("Specific Personal Information"), the "Act on the Use of Numbers to Identify a Specific Individual in Administrative Procedures" (the "Number Act") applies as a special law of APPI (See XXIV).

VII. Extraterritorial Application

1. Collection in Relation to the Offering of Goods or Services

Article 75 of APPI stipulates that the provisions (except for a few provisions[4]) regarding the obligations of the business operator apply to the business operator when it handles in a foreign country the personal data of data subjects who are in Japan collected in relation to providing goods or services to such data subjects (75). This business operator is not limited to the business operator who has an office etc. in Japan but also includes a foreign company which has no office etc. in Japan.

Therefore, Article 75 of APPI would be substantially the same as paragraph 2 (a), Article 3 of GDPR, which stipulates that GDPR applies to the processing of personal data of data subjects who are in the Union (EU) by a controller or processor not established in the Union in relation to the offering of goods or services to such data subjects. In fact, the General GL states that APPI applies when a foreign company offers goods or services over the Internet to Japanese consumers and collects their personal information to send or provide the goods or services, and when a foreign e-mail service provider collects Japanese users' personal information for setting their accounts, etc. (p.82).

---

[4] The following provisions do Not apply to the business operator when it handles in a foreign country the personal data of data subjects who are in Japan collected in relation to providing goods or services to such data subjects (See 75):
  (a) Article 26: the obligations of the business operator who receives personal data from a third party to confirm certain items (including the circumstances under which the third party obtained the personal data) and make and maintain the record of the confirmation.
  (b) Articles 37 through 39: the provisions regarding anonymously processed information.
  (c) Articles 40: PPC's authority to conduct an on-site investigation and request production of documents.

2. Application to the Monitoring of Data Subjects

In contrast, there is no such provision like paragraph 2 (b) of Article 3 of GDPR, which stipulates that GDPR applies to the monitoring of the behavior of data subjects who are in the Union by a controller or processor not established in the Union. However, when the business operator who does not have any office etc. in Japan monitors the behavior of data subjects who are in Japan and collects their personal data, at least Article 17 (proper collection) and Article 18 (2) (notification of the purpose of use when collecting personal data described in a written contract or other documents directly from the data subject) would apply because the important part of the collection is done in Japan (See General GL p81).

VIII. Principles Relating to Handling of Personal Data

In relation to Chapter II (Principles) of GDPR, APPI has the following provisions.

1. Restriction of Collection

The business operator shall not collect personal information by deception or other wrongful means (17(1)) (e.g. to collect personal information notifying the data subject of a false purpose of use: General GL p.32).

2. Prohibition of Collecting Personal Information Requiring Special Consideration

The business operator shall not collect personal information requiring special consideration without obtaining the data subject's prior consent, except in any of the following cases (17(2), General GL p.33-35). The cases (a) through (d) are referred to as the "**general exceptional cases**" in this book.

(a) When the handling (including the collection, use, deletion, and provision of personal information; the same in (b) through (d) below) is required or authorized under laws or regulations.
[e.g. collection by an employer of the results of health check of its employees from hospitals under the Industrial Safety and Health Act]
(b) When the handling is necessary to protect the data subject's life, body or property and it is difficult to obtain his or her consent.
[e.g. collection by a doctor or nurse of the data subject's clinical history from his or her family when the data subject was seriously injured]
(c) When the handling is particularly necessary for the improvement of public health or the promotion of healthy development of children and it is difficult to obtain the data subject's consent.
[e.g. collection of medical examination results for epidemiological studies, or collection of information on the suspicion of child abuse by the child consultation center, police, school or hospital from the other organization]
(d) When the handling is necessary to cooperate with a central government organization or a local government, or a person entrusted by them in their executing their legal duties and obtaining the data subject's consent is likely to impede the execution of such duties.
[e.g. collection of personal data of others to respond to a voluntary inquiry from the police]
(e) When the personal information requiring special consideration has been disclosed to the public by the data subject; a central government organization; a local government; a news media, writer, academic organization, religious organization or political organization, etc. (as far as the disclosure had been done for news report, writing, academic studies, religious activities or political activities, etc.); or other persons specified by the Rules.

(f) In the case prescribed by the Order as equivalent to any of the foregoing cases.

3. **Specification and Restriction of Purpose of Use (Purpose Limitation)**

(a) The business operator shall, when handling personal information, specify the purpose of use thereof as specific as possible (the "purpose of use") (15(1)).
(b) The business operator who owns retained personal data shall make certain information (including the purpose of use) easily accessible to the data subject or disclose the same at his or her request without delay (27) (See IX-1-(2)).
(c) The business operator, when collecting personal data described in a document directly from the data subject, shall clearly indicate to the data subject the purpose of use prior to the collection (18(2)) (See IX-1-(1)).
(d) Except in the case (c) above, when the business operator collected personal information, it shall notify the data subject of, or disclose to the public the purpose of use promptly after the collection unless the business operator had already disclosed it to the public (18(1)) (See IX-1-(1)).
(e) The business operator shall not handle the personal information beyond the scope necessary to achieve the purpose of use without obtaining the data subject's prior consent, except in any of the general exceptional cases (16(1), (3)).
(f) The business operator shall not change the purpose of use beyond the scope reasonably relevant to the purpose of use before the change, without obtaining the data subject's prior consent (15(2)) (in other words, beyond the scope that the data subject should normally expect from the purpose of use before the change; General GL p. 27).
(g) When the business operator has collected personal information by succeeding another business operator's business in the form of a merger or others, it shall not handle the personal information beyond the scope

necessary to achieve the purpose of use before the succession of the business, except in any of the general exceptional cases (16(2), (3)).
(h) When the business operator has changed the purpose of use, it shall notify the data subject of the changed purpose of use or disclose the same to the public (18(3)) (See IX-1-(1)).

Examples of (a) above (General GL p.26)
a) A good example of the specification: "to provide information on new products of our XYZ business"
b) A bad example of the specification: "for marketing purpose"

Examples of (f) above (Q&A p.17)
a) The change of the purpose of use that does not need the data subject's prior consent:
   - The change from "to provide information on our products" to "to provide information on our products and our alliance partners' services"
b) The change of the purpose of use that needs the data subject's prior consent:
   - The change to add the provision of the personal data to a third party; or
   - The change from "for the communication when the membership card is stolen" to "…. and for providing information on our services"

4. Accuracy and the Deletion of Unnecessary Personal Data

The business operator shall endeavor to keep personal data accurate and up-to-date to the extent necessary to achieve the purpose of use and delete the personal data without delay after its use became no longer necessary (19).

5. Obligations in Relation to Providing or Receiving Personal Data

(1). **The Principle of the Data Subject's Consent**

The business operator shall not provide personal data to a third party (in Japan) without obtaining the data subject's prior consent (23(1)), except in any of the general exceptional cases and of the cases described in (2) and (3) below. With respect to the restriction on the provision of personal data to a third party in a foreign country, Article 24 applies (See XX). Making personal data accessible or available to a third party constitutes the "provision" of the personal data to the third party (General GL p.25).

The General GL gives the following (p.45):
(a) as the examples that fall under the provision of personal data to a third party: exchange of personal data among affiliated companies or between a franchisor and its franchisees; and
(b) as the example that does Not fall under the provision of personal data to a third party: exchange of personal data between different departments in a same single entity.

(2). Provision to a Third Party Using Opt-out Mechanism

The business operator may provide personal data (excluding personal information requiring special consideration) to a third party (in Japan) without obtaining the data subject's prior consent when all the following conditions are satisfied (23(2), Rule 7 through 10, General GL p.48,49):

(a) The business operator shall, before the provision to the third party, a) notify the data subjects of all the following items or make them easily accessible to the data subjects [e.g. posting them in the location on the business operator's website which the data subject easily finds] and b) report to PPC all the following items;
   (i) that the purpose of use includes the provision to the third party
   [Note: This means the purpose of use which the business operator has made accessible, disclosed, indicated, or notified to the data subjects or has disclosed to the public under APPI (27, 18(1) or

18(2)) (See IX-1) must include the provision to the third party.]
- (ii) the items of the personal data which the business operator will provide to the third party
[e.g. a name, address, telephone number, age, purchase history]
- (iii) the way to provide the personal data to the third party
[e.g. by electronic information communication means or delivery of recording media]
- (iv) that the business operator will discontinue the provision to the third party upon request from the data subject, and
- (v) the way to receive the request from the data subject to discontinue the provision
[e.g. by mail, e-mail or input on a website]
- (b) After (a) above, PPC shall publish the information relating to the items in (a), using the Internet or other appropriate measures;
- (c) After (b) above, the business operator shall publish all the items in (a) above, using the Internet or other appropriate measures;
- (d) If the data subject requests the business operator not to provide or discontinue providing his or her personal data to the third party, the business operator shall comply with the request; and
- (e) Only after a reasonable period during which the data subject may make the request mentioned in (d) above elapsed, the business operator may provide the personal data to the third party.

The conditions (a) through (e) above also apply when the business operator intends to change the items (ii), (iii) or (v) in (a) above (23(3), (4)).

If the business operator in a foreign country intends to provide personal data to a third party (in Japan) using the opt-out mechanism, it shall designate a representative in Japan to have the representative do the report to PPC mentioned in (a) above or the preceding sentence (Rule 8).

This exemption (the "**Opt-out Mechanism**") was introduced in APPI since its first enactment in 2003. One of the reasons is that in Japan, land-line telephone user directories, Who's Who, lists of individual members of alumni associations, business organizations, or other organizations, etc. had been distributed and used without any special limitation for a long time; and maps containing names collected from doorplates of individuals' houses and shapes of their houses had been sold and widely used since the 1950s for a wide range of activities, including the maintenance and preservation of lifelines such as electricity, gas and water, the disaster prevention, the protection of life and property by the fire department and police, and the services in everyday life such as postal delivery and home delivery.

(3). <u>Exceptions in the Cases of Entrustment of Handling, Merger, Joint-Use, Etc.</u>

In any of the following cases, the party which receives the personal data from the business operator (the "receiving party") is not deemed to be the "third party," to which above obligations apply (23(5)). Accordingly, in such a case, the business operator may provide the personal data to the receiving party without obtaining the data subject's prior consent and without using the opt-out mechanism:

(a) When the business operator provides the personal data to the receiving party to entrust the handling the personal data in whole or in part;
[e.g. the provision of personal data to the receiving party to outsource information processing or delivery of goods (General GL p.52)]
(b) When the receiving party receives the personal data in a merger or other form of the succession of a business from the business operator;
(c) When the business operator jointly uses the personal data with the receiving party (both are herein called the "joint user(s)"). In this case, the business operator shall, before the provision, notify the data subject of all the

following items or make them easily accessible to the data subject:
(i) the intended provision,
(ii) the categories of the personal data to be used jointly,
(iii) the scope of other joint user(s),
(iv) the purpose(s) of use of the other joint user(s), and
(v) the name of the joint user primarily responsible for the management of the personal data.

The General GL (p.53) gives as an example of the joint use the one between affiliated companies. It should be noted that the purpose of use of the receiving party must be included in the purpose of use which the business operator has disclosed under APPI (27,18(1) or 18(2)) (General GL p.52). The General GL states it is desirable for the joint-users to have an agreement on the management of the joint-use in advance (p.54).

(4). Record Obligations Concerning Providing or Receiving Personal Data

Large-scale leakage of personal information became public in July 2014. The leakage was from Benesse Corporation, one of the largest correspondence education service providers for children. An employee of an affiliated company of Benesse which had been operating a database on behalf of Benesse unlawfully brought out personal information such as names, addresses, phone numbers, sex, dates of birth, etc. of the children and/or their guardians. He sold the information to a so-called "Meibo-ya," whose business is to sell various kinds of directories and other personal information. The number of the data subjects of the leaked data was reportedly about 28.95 million.

After this incident, it came to be said that the deterrence of unethical Meibo-ya was necessary. As a result, under the amended APPI, when the business operator provided personal data to a third party (in Japan or a foreign country) or when it receives personal data from a third party (in Japan or a foreign country), it is obliged to do the following.

(a) Record Obligations When Provided Personal Data

(i) The business operator, when provided personal data to a third party, shall make a record of the following items and maintain it for a certain period (one or three years) (25, Rules 13, 14):
   a) the name of the third party (or other information by which the third party can be identified, or if the personal data were provided to unspecified third parties, that fact);
   b) the name of the data subject identified by the personal data (or other information by which the data subject can be identified);
   c) the items of the personal data (e.g. a name, address, telephone number, age, purchase history);
   d) if the personal data were provided using the opt-out mechanism, the date of the provision; and
   a) if the personal data were provided based on the data subject's consent under Article 23 or Article 24 (the provision to a third party in a foreign country), that such consent has been obtained.

The business operator is not required to make the record:
   a) in the case where the third party is the public institution;
   b) in any of the general exceptional cases; or
   c) if the third party is in Japan, in the case of the entrustment of the handling of personal data, the merger or other successions of a business, or the joint use of personal data which are mentioned in (3) above.

In the case where the items to be recorded are stated in a written agreement executed for the provision of the personal data, the business operator may use the agreement as the record (Rule 12(3)).

(ii) The business operator shall not give any false information when the third party confirms certain items described in (b) below (26(2)).

(b) Record Obligations When Receiving Personal Data

(i) The business operator, when receiving personal data from a third party, shall confirm the following items by the following methods (26(1), Rule 15):

a) the name of the third party (and if the third party is a company or any other body, the name of its representative director or other representative), by receiving declarations form the third party or any other appropriate method; or

b) the circumstances under which the third party collected the personal data (e.g. from whom and how to), by receiving a copy of the contract that indicates such circumstances or any other appropriate method.

(ii) The business operator shall, when so confirmed, make a record of the following items and maintain it for a certain period (one or three years) (26 (3), (4), Rules 17,18):

b) the name of the third party (and if the third party is a company or any other body, the name of its representative director or other representative);

c) the circumstances under which the third party collected the personal data (e.g. from whom and how to);

d) the name of the data subject identified by the personal data (or other information by which the data subject can be identified);

e) the items of the personal data (e.g. a name, address, telephone number, age, purchase history);

f) if the personal data were provided using the opt-out mechanism, the date of receiving the personal data, and that PPC had published the

information relating to the items to be reported by the third party, and
g) if the personal data were provided based on the data subject's consent under Article 23 or Article 24 (provision to a third party in a foreign country), that such consent has been obtained.

The business operator is not required to make the record:
a) in any of the general exceptional cases; or
b) in the case of the entrustment of handling of personal data, the merger or other succession of a business or the joint use of personal data which are mentioned in (3) above.

In the case where the items to be recorded are stated in a written agreement executed for the provision of the personal data, the business operator may use the agreement as the record (Rule 16(3)).

When the business operator received the personal data even though it suspected the personal data had been collected not lawfully, it might constitute the violation of the prohibition of collection by wrongful means under Article 17 of APPI (Confirmation and Record GL p.13).

(5). Use of Cloud Services

The meaning of the "provision" to a third party of personal data in the context of using cloud services is explained in several answers in Q&A (A5-33, A5-34, A9-5, and A9-6).

Considering these answers together, regardless of whether the cloud server or the cloud service provider is in Japan or a foreign country, if both of the conditions (a) and (b) below are satisfied, the cloud service provider is Not deemed to be handling the personal data stored by the cloud service user on the cloud server. As a result, in this case, such storage or use by the user is not deemed to constitute the "provision" of the personal data to the provider (a third party) in Japan (23) or in a foreign country (24).

(a) It is stipulated in a contract between the provider and the user that the provider shall not handle the personal data; and
(b) Access control is properly performed.

Here, the meaning of "Access control is properly performed" in condition (b) above is not clear. However, it would mean that the user is using IDs, passwords, encryption, or other means to prevent any unauthorized access by third parties including the provider, or that access by the provider is not possible due to the design of the cloud service.

If both the above conditions are satisfied, the restriction of the provision of personal data to a third party in APPI (23 and 24) (e.g. obligations of obtaining data subject's consent and record or confirmation) would not apply.

At the same time, in this case, as the cloud service provider is Not deemed to be handling the personal data stored by the cloud service user on the cloud server, the user is Not considered to entrust the provider with the handling of the personal data. Therefore, in this case, the user is not subject to the obligation that a business operator shall supervise the third party to which the business operator entrusted the handling of the personal data (22).

In contrast, if any of the conditions (a) and (b) above is Not satisfied (e.g. where the provider undertakes the analysis of a database of the user's individual customers), the user is considered to entrust the provider with the handling of the personal data, and therefore, needs to supervise the provider to ensure the security of the personal data (22). However, in this case, if the provider is established in Japan, as mentioned in (3) above, the user is not required to obtain the data subject's consent to provide his or her personal data to the provider (23(5)). With respect to the user's obligation to supervise the provider, if the provider has a certification of the compliance with reliable security standards (e.g. those of ISO), the user would be considered to fulfill the supervisory obligation by confirming the certification even if the user does not have an audit right.

With respect to the use of a foreign company's cloud service, further consideration is given in XX.

6. Difference from GDPR

The major differences of APPI from GDPR are as follows:

(a) GDPR has Article 5 (principles relating to the processing of personal data), which stipulates the following principles: lawfulness; fairness and transparency; purpose limitation; data minimization; accuracy; storage limitation; integrity and confidentiality; and accountability. APPI does not have such single provision that generally states principles of handling personal data, and it does not have provisions that clearly state the principles of data minimization and accountability.

(b) Under GDPR, processing of personal data is lawful only under one of the legal bases specified in Article 6, such as the data subject's prior consent, or the controller's legitimate interest not overridden by the interests or fundamental rights and freedoms of the data subject. In contrast, under APPI, such legal bases are not required for the collection or the use itself, except for the data subject's consent required for (i) the collection of personal information requiring special consideration (17(2)), (ii) the handling of personal information beyond the scope necessary to achieve the purpose of use (16(1)), (iii) the change of the purpose of use beyond the scope reasonably relevant to the purpose of use before the change (15(2)), and (iv) the provision of personal data to a third party in Japan (23(1)) or in a foreign country (24).

(c) Under GDPR, the consent of a data subject must be an unambiguous (4(11),7) or explicit (9(2),22(1)(c),49(1)(a)) indication of the data subject's wishes. Under APPI, such condition is not specifically required even for the collection of personal information requiring special consideration, therefore, the consent could be implicit or implied depending on the situation (Q&A A1-57).

(d) Under GDPR, the data subject shall have the right to withdraw his or her consent at any time (7(3)). In APPI, such withdrawal right is not stipulated.

(e) Under GDPR, where processing is based on consent, the controller shall be able to demonstrate that the data subject has consented to the processing of his or her personal data (7(1)). In APPI, such obligation is not stipulated.

(f) Article 8 of GDPR stipulates the special conditions applicable to children's consent in relation to information society services, including the authorization by the holder of parental responsibility for the child. APPI does not stipulate any such condition in relation to children's consent, while according to Q&A (A1-58), in general, if the data subject is 12-15 years or younger, the consent of his or her parent or other guardian is required.

(g) Under APPI, the business operator may provide personal data (excluding personal information requiring special consideration) to a third party in Japan without obtaining the data subject's prior consent (i) by using the opt-out mechanism, or (ii) in the case of the entrustment of the handling of personal data, merger or other forms of succession of a business, or joint use of personal data, as mentioned above. GDPR does not have such provisions.

IX. **Transparency: Information Disclosure to the Data Subject**

1. Business Operator's Obligations

(1). Disclosure Concerning the Collection of Personal Data and the Change of the Purpose of Use

1) When Collecting Personal Data Directly from the Data Subject in Writing

The business operator, when collecting personal data described in a written contract or other document (including that in an electronic form) directly from the data subject in conjunction with the execution of the contract with the data subject or otherwise, shall clearly indicate to the data subject the purpose of use prior to the collection, except when the business operator urgently needs to collect the personal data to protect the data subject's life, body or property (18(2)). [e.g. Before collecting personal data from an application form or the input on a website, the purpose of use shall be already printed on the application form or displayed on the website (See General GL p.37)]

2) When Collected Personal Data in the Case Other Than 1) Above

In this case, the business operator shall notify the data subject of the purpose of use or disclose the same to the public (e.g. by posting on its website) promptly after the collection, unless it has already disclosed the same to the public prior to the collection (18(1)).

3) When Changed the Purpose of Use

When the business operator has changed the purpose of use, it shall notify the data subject of the changed purpose of use or disclose the same to the public (18(3)).

It should be noted that if the purpose after the change is not within the scope reasonably relevant to the purpose of use before the change, the business operator shall obtain the data subject's consent prior to the change (15(2)).

4) Exemption from the Disclosure Obligations

The business operator is not required to disclose the purpose of use as mentioned in 1), 2) and 3) above in any of the following cases (18(4), General GL p.38,39):

(a) When there is a risk of harming the life, body, property or other rights or interests of the data subject or a third party due to the disclosure;
[e.g. When a child consultation center has the information that the data subject has abused his or her child]

(b) When the disclosure is likely to damage the rights or legitimate interests of the business operator;
[e.g. When a company, in order not to transact with a gang member, obtained information that the data subject is the member]

(c) When the business operator needs to cooperate with a central government organization or local government in their executing their legal duties and the disclosure is likely to impede the execution of such duties; or
[e.g. When the business operator received from the police personal information of a suspect of a crime to cooperate with their investigation]

(d) When the purpose of use is obvious from the circumstances of the collection.
[e.g. When exchanging business cards, it is obvious to use the contact information on the card for future communication (but not for sending direct mails)]

(2). Disclosure Concerning Retained Personal Data

With respect to retained personal data, the business operator shall make all the following information accessible to the data subject or disclose the same at his or her request without delay (27, Order 8):

(a) the business operator's name;
(b) the purpose(s) of use of all the retained personal data owned by the business operator;
(c) the procedures and ways of the request by the data subject for the disclosure, correction, addition or deletion, discontinuance of the use or deletion, or discontinuance

of providing to a third party of the personal data, and of the response by the business operator to that request; and

(d) the contact information for the data subject to lodge a complaint with the business operator concerning its handling of the retained personal data.

2. Difference from GDPR

The major differences of APPI from GDPR are as follows:

(a) Under APPI, the business operator shall disclose the purpose of use etc., but is not required to disclose other information specified in Articles 13 and 14 of GDPR, including; the legal basis for the processing, the period for which the personal data will be stored, data subject's rights to the controller and right to lodge a complaint with a supervisory authority; whether the data subject is obliged to provide the personal data and the possible consequences of failure to provide such data; and the existence of automated decision-making, including profiling.

(b) APPI has no such specific requirements as those in GDPR concerning the manner of disclosing the information (such as "in a concise, transparent, intelligible and easily accessible form, using clear and plain language…in writing…") (GDPR 12) or the timing or deadline of disclosing the information (where personal data relating to a data subject are collected from the data subject, at the time when personal data are obtained (GDPR 13), and where personal data have not been obtained from the data subject, at the latest within one month (GDPR 14)).

X. Rights of the Data Subject

1. Right to Request Disclosure (Right of Access)

The data subject may request the business operator to disclose the retained personal data of him or her that the business operator has or the purpose of use, except in certain cases, such as where there is a risk of harming the life, body, property or other rights or interests of the data subject or a third party due to the disclosure (28(1), 27(2)).

2. Right to Request Correction

The data subject may request the business operator to correct, add other information to, or delete the retained personal data if the data is not factual (29(1)). There is no substantial difference from Article 16 (Right to rectification) of GDPR.

3. Right to Request Discontinuance of the Use or the Provision to a Third Party

The data subject may request the business operator to discontinue the use of or delete the retained personal data in either case of (a) or (b) below (30(1)):
(a) when the business operator collected the retained personal data by deception or other wrongful means, or
(b) when the business operator handled the retained personal data beyond the scope necessary to achieve the purpose of use without obtaining the data subject's prior consent.

If the business operator provided the retained personal data to a third-party in Japan or a foreign country in violation of Article 23 or 24 of APPI, the data subject may request the business operator to discontinue the provision (30(3)).

4. Difference from GDPR

The major differences of APPI from GDPR are as follows:

(a) APPI has no provision concerning the items to be disclosed other than the content of the data or the purpose of use, like those stipulated in Article 15 of GDPR (e.g. the existence of data subject's rights, the source of collection).
(b) APPI has no provision on the following rights like GDPR.
 (i) the right to withdraw the consent (GDPR 7(3))
 (ii) the right to data portability (GDPR 20)
 (iii) the right to object (GDPR 21)
 (iv) the right not to be subject to a decision based solely on automated processing (22).
(c) Under GDPR, the data subject may request the controller to discontinue the use of or delete or discontinue the provision to a third party of his or her personal data with substantially no condition, by using the rights in (i), (iii) or (iv) in (b) above. But APPI limits the conditions as mentioned above.

5. The Nature of the Data Subject's Rights

Before the amendment, APPI only had a provision which stated, "the business operator…shall disclose (or correct or discontinue using) the personal data … when requested by the data subject…" (25, 26 and 27).

Thus, there was a court judgment stating; It is difficult to interpret that this provision gives the data subject a legal right. Therefore, the data subject may not enforce his or her request through the judicial proceedings (the judgment of the Tokyo District Court on June 27, 2007).

However, amended APPI clarified that the data subject is given the legal rights by stating "The data subject may request (disclosure etc.)" (28, 29, 30).

Amended APPI also clarified the conditions under which the data subject may exercise the rights through the judicial proceedings by stipulating; The data subject may file a lawsuit to exercise the rights after (i) the lapse of two weeks from his or her request to the business operator for disclosure etc., or (ii) the business operator's rejection to the request, whichever comes first (34(1)).

6. Right to Be Forgotten

In Japan, there was a lower court judgment that recognized the right to be forgotten. However, as summarized below, the Supreme Court decision on January 31, 2017, stated that there can be a case where this right is recognized, but set strict requirements, and, in this case, denied the right.

(1). Background

This decision is the Supreme Court decision concerning a petition for a provisional disposition order. When the petitioner (appellant) performed a search with Google search engine after entering his name etc., an article that reported he had been arrested for child prostitution in the past was displayed as one of the search results. He petitioned for a provisional disposition order for Google to discontinue displaying such search result.

(2). Summary of the Supreme Court Decision

The provision of search results has an aspect of expression as the search engine is designed to obtain certain results in line with the policy of the search engine provider. The provision of search results also plays a key role as a basis for distribution of information on the Internet in modern societies. Although the individual's privacy is subject to legal protection, forcing deletion of such search results is a constraint on freedom of expression and said key role.

The request to discontinue displaying such search results shall be accepted when it is apparent that the petitioner's interest that the fact of the arrest is not disclosed to the public overrides the interest derived from the disclosure of the fact, considering the nature of the facts searched; the degree of damage to the petitioner's privacy; and the purpose and importance of the information, etc.

When applying these considerations to this case, the child prostitution should be strongly condemned and still is a concern which relates to the public interest, and the fact of the arrest is only a part of the search results. Therefore, the override (priority) of the petitioner's interest is not apparent.

(3). The Legal Basis of the Right to Be Forgotten

The petition and appeal were based on the privacy right that is said to be derived from the right of pursuit of happiness under Article 13 of the Japanese Constitution, not a right under APPI.

The reason for this would be that even under amended APPI, the data subject may request discontinuance of the use or deletion of the retained personal data only in one of the above-mentioned cases (i.e. the collection by deception or other wrongful means, or the handling beyond the scope necessary to achieve the purpose of use without obtaining the data subject's prior consent), but a typical case where the right to be forgotten is sought (like the petition above) does not fall under any of such cases.

XI. Measures and Certification of Compliance

APPI has no provisions like GDPR concerning implementation of appropriate data protection policies (24(2)); demonstration of compliance by adherence to approved codes of conduct (24(3)); data protection by design and by default (25); codes of conduct (40); and data protection certification mechanisms and data protection seals and marks (42).

However, as APPI requires the business operator to take necessary and appropriate measures to ensure the security of personal data (20), the implementation of appropriate data protection policies etc. are normally required or can be used (General GL p.87-98).

XII. No Requirement to Designate a Representative in Japan

Under GDPR, if a controller or processor is not established in EU but is subject to the extraterritorial application, it shall designate a representative in EU (27(1), (3)). In contrast, APPI does not have such requirement, provided, however, that if the business operator in a foreign country intends to provide personal data to a third party (in Japan) using the opt-out mechanism, it shall designate a representative in Japan to have the representative do the report to PPC (Rule8).

XIII. Entrustment of the Handling of Personal Data to a Third Party

Under APPI, the business operator, when entrusting a third party with the handling of the personal data in whole or in part, shall supervise the third party to ensure the security of personal data (22).
However, APPI does not have any specific provision like Article 28 of GDPR on the conditions concerning the selection of such third party, restriction of subcontracting, the legal form and content of the contract with the third party, and the standard contractual clauses for the contract, while the General GL (p.43) refers to the selection of and the contract with the third party.

XIV. The Obligation to Record the Handling of Personal Data

APPI does not have such provision as Article 30 of GDPR, which requires a controller or processor to maintain a record of processing activities generally. However, as explained in VIII-5, when the business operator provides personal data to a third party or receives personal data from a third party, APPI imposes certain record obligations (26).

XV. Security of Handling

1. Basic Principles

The business operator shall take necessary and appropriate security measures to prevent possible leakage or loss of, or damage to personal data (20).

2. Supervision of Employees or a Third Party

The business operator shall, to ensure the security of personal data, exercise necessary and appropriate supervision over (i) employees (including officers) when having them handle the personal data (21, General GL p.42), and (ii) a third party when entrusting it with the handling of the personal data (22).

3. A Summary of PPC's Recommendations on Security Measures

The measures summarized below are recommended to take as an example of appropriate security measures in the General GL (p.86-98).

(a) Establishment of basic policies.
(b) Establishment of internal rules on the handling of personal data, including the following measures in (c) through (f) below.
(c) Organizational Security Measures.
    a) Establishment of the organizational structure.
    b) Recording of the handling.
    c) Identification of the personal data, their purposes of use, responsible persons and departments, etc.
    d) Establishment of measures to be taken in the event of leakage etc.

e) Inspection, audit, and review of the status of the handling and the security measures.
- (d) Human-related Security Measures
   a) Training of employees.
   b) Providing confidentiality obligation in employment regulations.
- (e) Physical Security Measures
   a) Control of the entry and exit of areas handling personal data, and restriction of devices which can be brought in.
   b) Safekeeping of devices or media in a lockable cabinet etc.
   c) Prevention of leakage etc. when carrying devices or media, etc. by encryption, password, etc.
   d) Deletion of personal data and disposal of devices or media by secure methods.
- (f) Technical Security Measures
   a) Access control
      - Limitation of the information systems, databases, and employees which or who can access personal data.
      - Authentication of access by an ID, password, magnetic card, IC card, etc.
   b) Prevention and detection of unauthorized access from the outside, by the firewall, antivirus software, automatic update of software, regular analysis of logs, etc.
   c) Security at the time of designing the information system and its continuous review.
   d) Protection by encryption, password, etc. during communication or transmission of data.

4. Difference from GDPR

(a) GDPR specifically refers to pseudonymization and encryption as one of appropriate technical and organizational measures to ensure the security (32(1)(a)). While APPI does not specifically refer to them, they may be chosen as appropriate measures for the security even under APPI.

(b) Under GDPR, the controller and the processor shall take into consideration the security risk and assess the appropriate level of security in implementing appropriate technical and organizational measures (32(1), (2)). While APPI has no specific reference to such consideration and assessment, they should be employed by the business operator even under APPI.

(c) GDPR stipulates that adherence to an approved code of conduct or an approved certification mechanism may be used as an element to demonstrate the implementation of appropriate technical and organizational security measures (32(3)). APPI does not have such provision, as it does not impose such demonstration obligation on the business operator.

XVI. Notification of Data Leakage Etc. to the Supervisory Authority and Data Subjects

Under GDPR, in the case of a personal data breach (a breach of security leading to the accidental or unlawful destruction, loss, alteration, unauthorised disclosure of, or access to, personal data) (4(12)), the controller shall notify the breach to the competent supervisory authority (33(1)), and if the breach is likely to result in a high risk to the rights and freedoms of natural persons, the controller shall communicate the breach to the data subjects (34(1)).

APPI does not have such provisions that directly require such notification or communication. However, the "Measures to Be Taken in the Event of Leakage Etc. of Personal Data" (the "Measures in the Case of Data Leakage") published by PPC states that it is desirable for the business operator to report leakage or other similar incidents to PPC and notify them to the data subjects who are potentially affected.

<Outline of the Measures in the Case of Data Leakage>

(1) Leakage etc. to which the measures apply

The measures apply to any of the following (the "leakage etc."):
(a) the leakage or loss of, or damage to personal data,
(b) the leakage of the deleted information or the processing, or
(c) the likelihood of (a) or (b) above.

(2) Measures to be taken when the leakage etc. is found

It is desirable for the business operator to take the following measures:
(a) reporting within the business operator's organization and prevention of expansion of the damage;
(b) factual investigation and identification of the causes;
(c) identification of the extent of the impact;
(d) development and implementation of recurrence prevention measures;
(e) notification to the data subjects who may be affected depending on the level of anticipated impact; and
(f) publication of the facts and causes and the recurrence prevention measures.

(3) Report to PPC

The business operator should endeavor to report the facts found, the measures to prevent reoccurrence, etc. to PPC promptly, except in any case where:
(a) It can be virtually said that the personal data, or the deleted information or the processing methods of the anonymously processed information (the "data etc.") are not leaked to the outside of the business operator, because;
   a) The data etc. had been encrypted before the leakage etc.;
   b) The data etc. have been collected before being accessed by any third party;
   c) It is impossible for anyone other than the

business operator to identify specific individuals from the data etc.; or
- d) The leakage etc. involves only the deletion of the data etc.

(b) The leakage etc. is only the misdirection of facsimile messages or e-mails or the misdelivery of goods with a minor impact.

XVII. No Requirement for Data Protection Impact Assessment (DPIA)

Under GDPR, (i) where a type of processing is likely to result in a high risk, the controller shall, prior to the processing, carry out an assessment of the impact of the envisaged processing (35(1)), and (ii) where the assessment indicates that the processing would result in a high risk in the absence of measures taken by the controller to mitigate the risk, the controller shall, prior to processing, consult the supervisory authority (36(1)).

APPI does not have such provisions.

XVIII. No Requirement to Designate a Data Protection Officer (DPO)

Under GDPR, the controller and processor shall appoint a data protection officer (DPO) in certain cases (37(1)), including where:

(a) the core activities of the controller or the processor consist of processing operations which require regular and systematic monitoring of data subjects on a large scale; or

(b) the core activities of the controller or the processor consist of processing on a large scale of special categories of data and personal data relating to criminal convictions and offenses.

APPI does not have such provision. However, appointing the person who is responsible for handling personal information in the business operator is listed in the General GL (p.89) as one of the appropriate measures for security.

XIX. Codes of Conduct and Certification Mechanism

1. Codes of Conduct

An association of business operators accredited by PPC[5] shall endeavor to prepare guidelines for the protection of personal information, and when prepared, report it to PPC, and PPC shall publish the guidelines (53).

The association, when received a complaint from a data subject concerning its member's handling of his or her personal information, shall consult with and give necessary advice to the data subject, conduct necessary investigation, and notify the complaint and request a prompt resolution to that member (52(1)). The member shall not reject the request without a justifiable reason (52(3)).

2. Certification Mechanism

Under GDPR, the establishment of data protection certification mechanisms and of data protection seals and marks are encouraged for demonstrating compliance with GDPR (42).

APPI does not have a provision that directly refers to such mechanisms. However, in Japan, as further explained below, (i) there is a privacy mark system that started before the enactment of APPI in 2003, and (ii) it is possible to obtain

---

[5] The list of the associations of business operators accredited by PPC: https://www.ppc.go.jp/personal/nintei/list/

a certification under the Cross-Border Privacy Rules (CBPR) of Asia-Pacific Economic Cooperation (APEC).

(1). The Outline of Privacy Mark System in Japan

The privacy mark system is a system that certifies the business operator that is taking appropriate measures to protect personal information in compliance with the Japanese Industrial Standards (JIS) Q 15001 "Personal Information Protection Management System - Requirements" and grants the business operator to use an approved privacy mark[6]. JIPDEC, an organization established under the guidance of the Ministry of Economy, Trade and Industry (METI) has been operating this system since 1998. The objectives of this system are as follows:

(a) to improve consumer awareness regarding the protection of personal information by a mark visible to consumers, and

(b) to provide businesses with incentives to respond to the growing consumers' consciousness of the protection of personal information by promoting proper handling thereof, and thereby earn society's credibility.

The privacy mark system is a system in which a third party objectively evaluates the personal information protection system of the business operator based on JIS Q 15001 which includes the requirements under APPI. Therefore, for the business operator, the mark is an effective tool to demonstrate that it has a system which not only complies with APPI but also protects personal information at a higher level.

(2). APEC CBPR (Cross-Border Privacy Rules)

With the globalization of business, APEC established and has been operating the CBPR system[7] to properly

---

[6] The Privacy Mark System, JIPDEC website
https://privacymark.jp/system/index.html

protect personal information transferred across borders. Under this system, companies (i) assess their own rules and systems for the protection of such personal information and (ii) have an accredited neutral organization (an "accountability agent") review the results of the assessment, and (iii) if certain requirements are confirmed to be satisfied, are given certifications. In March 2016, JIPDEC was approved to serve as an accountability agent and started the certification procedures in June of the same year[8].

Re
[7] CROSS BORDER PRIVACY RULES SYSTEM
http://www.cbprs.org/

[8] JIPDEC website
https://www.jipdec.or.jp/protection_org/cbpr/index.html

XX. Provision of Personal Data to a Third Party in a Foreign Country

1. The Principle of the Data Subject's Consent

The business operator (the "data exporter") shall, when providing personal data to a third party in a foreign country (the "data importer"), obtain the data subject's prior consent that specifically refers to the provision to a third party in a foreign country (24).

The "third party in a foreign country" here (Foreign GL p.5, 6):
(a) includes an affiliated company of the data exporter in a foreign country;
(b) does not include a branch office of the data exporter in a foreign country; and
(c) does not include a foreign company that handles a personal information database etc in Japan for use in business (e.g. where it has an office or is doing business in Japan).

Different from the restriction of the provision of the personal data to a third party in Japan (23), there is no exception in the case of the entrustment of handling of the personal data, merger or other forms of the business succession or joint use of the personal data. Therefore, obtaining the data subject's prior consent is required even in any of these cases.

However, obtaining the data subject's prior consent is Not required if the data importer is in the country that is accredited under the Rules as a country which has the level for protection of personal information equivalent to that of Japan. As of May 2018, no country is so accredited, while, as mentioned in XX-5, PPC and the European Commission are working towards achieving a simultaneous finding of an adequate level of protection by both sides.

The business operator, when provided personal data to a third party in a foreign country, shall make a record of the date of the provision, the name of the third party (or other information by which the third party can be identified, or if the personal data were provided to unspecified third parties, that fact), the name of the data subject identified by the personal data (or other information by which the data subject can be identified), the items of the personal data (e.g. a name, address, telephone number, age, purchase history), and the data subject's consent (if obtained) for a certain period (one or three years), except in any of the general exceptional case (25, Rules 13,14).

2. The Exception under a Contract or Internal Rules or an International Framework

In the case (a) or (b) below, the business operator (the data exporter) may provide personal data to a third party in a foreign country (the data importer) without obtaining the data subject's prior consent that specifically refers to the provision to a third party in a foreign country (24, Rules 11).

(a) When it is ensured by "adequate and reasonable means" between the data exporter and the data importer that the data importer shall continuously take the measures equivalent to those which the data exporter (or a business operator) should take under APPI concerning the handling of personal data.

<Examples of the "adequate and reasonable means"> (General GL p.7, 32)
a) When the data exporter entrusts the handling of personal data to the data importer:

A contract, memorandum of understanding, etc. between the data exporter and the data importer. It is, so to say, a Japanese version of the standard data protection clause (SDPC) under GDPR (46(2)(c),(d)) or the standard contractual clauses (SCC) under the EU Data Protection Directive (26(2)(4)).

b) When the data exporter and the data importer are in the same corporate group (i.e. affiliates):

Internal regulations, privacy policies, etc. that apply to the data exporter and the data importer. They are, so to say, Japanese versions of the Binding Corporate Rules (BCR) under GDPR (47).

However, the content and form of Japanese versions of SDPC, SCC, and BCR are neither standardized nor required to be authorized by a supervisory authority, rather it is enough if they include the data importer's obligations equivalent to those of the data exporter (or a business operator) under APPI. Foreign GL explains the provisions to be included in the Japanese versions of SDPC, SCC, and BCR.

(b) When the data exporter or the data importer has a certification under an international framework for the handling of personal information (e.g. APEC CBPR).

It should be noted, however, that even in the case (a) or (b) above, while it is not necessary to obtain the data subject's prior consent that specifically refers to the provision to a third party in a foreign country, the following conditions must be satisfied, in addition to or as preconditions of the "adequate and reasonable means" or the certification (See Foreign GL p.3,4):

(i) The data exporter, before the provision, a) has already obtained the consent of the data subject to the provision of his or her personal data to third parties in general (i.e. without specifically referring to a third party in a foreign country) (the "general consent") or b) has taken the procedures required under the opt-out mechanism for the personal data;

(ii) When the provision to the data importer is for the entrustment of the handling of personal data, the data exporter shall supervise the data importer to ensure the security of personal data (22); or

(iii) When the provision to the data importer is for joint use of the personal data with the data importer, the data exporter, before the provision, has notified the data subject of certain items concerning the joint use or made them easily accessible to the data subject (23(5)-3).

The is because there is no reason why the data exporter is exempt from the obligations mentioned in (i) through (iii) above, as APPI has set conditions for the provision to a third party in a foreign country stricter than those for the provision to a third party in Japan.

For example, if the data exporter has obtained its customers' general consent to the provision of their personal data to affiliates of the data exporter, but later comes to want to provide the personal data to an affiliate in a foreign country, the data exporter may do so by executing an appropriate contract with the affiliate. However, if the data exporter has not obtained even the general consent, it must newly obtain the data subject's consent that specifically refers to the provision to a third party in a foreign country.

Section XXVII shows the author's drafts of two Japanese versions of SCC for the provision of personal data from the business operator in Japan (the data exporter) to a third party in a foreign country (the data importer) as follows:
(i) " PERSONAL DATA PROVISION AGREEMENT" that corresponds to the SCC in which the data importer is a controller (i.e. the data importer handles the personal data for its own self), and
(ii) "AGREEMENT FOR ENTRUSTMENT OF HANDLING OF PERSONAL DATA" which corresponds to the SCC in which the data importer is a processor (i.e. the data importer handles the personal data on behalf of the data exporter).

3. **Use of a Foreign Company's Cloud Service**

What is mentioned in VIII-5(5) (Use of Cloud Services) also applies to the use of a foreign company's cloud service, except that the last paragraph needs to be modified as follows:

If the cloud service provider is deemed to be handling the personal data stored by the cloud service user on the cloud server (e.g. where the provider undertakes the analysis of a database of the user's individual customers), the user is considered to entrust the provider with the handling of the personal data, and therefore, needs to supervise the provider to ensure the security of the personal data (22). At the same time, in this case, if the provider is established in a foreign country, as it constitutes the provision of personal data to a third party in a foreign country, unless the country is accredited under the Rules as a country which has the level for protection of personal information equivalent to that of Japan, the user is required to (i) obtain the data subject's consent to provide his or her personal data to the provider or (ii) ensure by a Japanese version of SCC etc. that the provider shall continuously take the measures equivalent to those which a business operator should take under APPI concerning the handling of personal data (24). With respect to the user's obligation to supervise the provider, if the provider has a certification of the compliance with reliable security standards (e.g. those of ISO), the user would be considered to fulfill the supervisory obligation by confirming the certification even if the user does not have an audit right.

However, if the foreign company is handling a personal information database etc. in Japan for use in business (e.g. where it has an office or is doing business in Japan), it is not regarded as "a third party in a foreign country" (Foreign GL p.5).

Therefore, when the business operator stores personal data on a cloud server operated by a foreign service provider, if the provider has an office or is doing business in Japan, such storage is not regarded as the provision of the personal data to "a third party in a foreign country."

For example, as Amazon Web Services, Inc. of USA ("AWS") is providing cloud computing services, including to Japanese users with servers located in Japan, even if a Japanese user stores personal data on an AWS server located in a foreign country, it will not be regarded as the provision of the personal data to "a third party in a foreign country," and thereby not be subject to the restriction of the provision of personal data to a third party in a foreign country (24).

With respect to the user's obligation to supervise AWS to ensure the security of the personal data (22), as AWS has certifications of the compliance with reliable security standards (e.g. those of ISO), the user would be considered to fulfill the supervisory obligation by confirming the certifications even if the user does not have an audit right.

It should be noted, however, that if the user provides or allows access to the personal data stored on the AWS server to the user's affiliated company or others in a foreign country, the user shall be subject to the restriction of the provision of personal data to a third party in a foreign country (24), as it is an issue different from the relationship with AWS.

4. Difference from GDPR

(a) Under GDPR, the consent of the data subject is regarded as an exceptional means (one of "derogations for specific situations") of lawful transfer to the outside of EEA, and SDPC, SCC, and BCR are regarded as the means to be taken first (49(1)). In contrast, as mentioned above, under APPI, the consent of the data subject is the primary means of lawful transfer to the outside of Japan.

(b) Under GDPR, the subject of the restriction is the transfer to "a third country or an international organization" (46), and the "recipient" of the personal data transferred is irrespective of whether it is a third party or not (4(9)). Therefore, for example, the transfer from a headquarters in EU to its branch office in Japan is the subject of the restriction. In contrast, under APPI, the subject of the restriction is the provision to "a third party in a foreign country." Therefore, for example, the provision from a branch office in Japan to its headquarters in EU is not the subject of the restriction because the branch office and the headquarters are organizations within a same single legal entity, not "a third party" each other.

(c) According to Q&A and Foreign GL, under certain conditions, the storage or use of personal data on a third-party cloud service provider's server in a foreign country is not subject to the restriction of the provision of personal data to a third party in a foreign country. Under GDPR, there would be no interpretation like that.

5. Japan EU Negotiation Toward Mutual Adequacy Findings

With respect to the provision or transfer of personal data between Japan and EU, PPC and the European Commission are working towards achieving a simultaneous finding of an adequate level of protection by both sides[9].

XXI. Supervisory Authority

Under the jurisdiction of the Prime Minister, PPC was established on January 1, 2016, as the organization which independently exercises the supervisory authority under APPI (41-). PPC was established by reorganizing the commission responsible for the protection of the Individual Number, also known as My Number, a 12-digit number assigned to every Japanese citizen or every resident of

---

[9] European Commission, "Communication from the commission to the European Parliament and the Council" Brussels, 24.1.2018, COM (2018) 43 final, p.6
https://ec.europa.eu/commission/sites/beta-political/files/data-protection-communication-com.2018.43.3_en.pdf

- Ministry of Internal Affairs and Communications (of Japan): Request for Public Comment on the draft "Guidelines on the Act on the Protection of Personal Information (Handling of the Personal Data Transferred From EU Under the Finding of an Adequate Level of Protection)" (in Japanese language only)   http://search.e-gov.go.jp/servlet/Public?CLASSNAME=PCMMSTDETAIL&id=240000050&Mode=0

Japan falling under certain conditions used for taxation, social security, etc. under the Number Act (explained in XXIV). APPI states that PPC's tasks include the drafting of the government's basic policies, the supervision over business operators (including on-site investigations, requests for production of documents), the mediation on complaints lodged by a data subject to the business operator, etc. to protect the rights and interests of individuals, while considering the usefulness of personal information (60, 61).

PPC has the following powers:
(a) to give guidance or advice to the business operator on the handling of personal information or anonymously processed information (41);
(b) if the business operator violated any of certain provisions of APPI, to recommend stopping the violation or taking other corrective action, and if the business operator does not take the recommended action, to order to take the recommended action (42(1), (2)); and
(c) if the business operator violated any of certain provisions of APPI and there is an urgent need, to order to take a certain action, without giving any recommendation in advance (42(3)).

XXII. <u>Remedies, Liability, and Penalties</u>

1. <u>Relevant Provisions of APPI</u>

(a) The data subject may file a lawsuit against the business operator to exercise the rights to disclosure; correction, addition or deletion; discontinuance of the use or deletion; or discontinuance of the provision to a third party, of his or her personal data after (i) the lapse of two weeks from his or her request to the business operator for the disclosure etc., or (ii) the business operator's rejection to the request, whichever comes first (34(1)).

(b) The data subject would be able to claim damages caused by an infringement of his or her right under APPI based on Article 709 (Tort) of the Civil Code.

(c) When an officer, employee, etc. of the business operator or the business operator who is a natural person provided a third party with a personal information database etc to seek illegal interests of him or her or a third party, he or she is subject to a criminal penalty (83).

(d) A natural person who violated or failed to comply with the order of PPC is subject to criminal penalties (84-86). His or her employer who is either a natural person or a legal entity may also be subject to criminal penalties (87).

2. Difference from GDPR

(a) Under GDPR, the data subject shall have the right to mandate a not-for-profit body etc. to exercise his or her rights on his or her behalf (80). APPI has no such provision.

(b) GDPR stipulates administrative fines (83). APPI has no such provision.

XXIII. Anonymously Processed Information

1. Definition

The term "anonymously processed information" (also called as the "API" in this Section XXIII) means the information that can be produced by processing personal information so as neither to be able to identify a specific person nor to be able to restore the personal information, by deleting or replacing a part of the descriptions in the said personal information (2(9)).

2. Background and Objectives

As already stated:

In June 2013, East Japan Railway Company received criticism by the public in respect of privacy about the fact that it had provided to other company the record of passengers' getting on and off, although specific individuals could not be identified by the record.

In November of the same year, NTT DoCoMo, a mobile telecommunications carrier, received criticism by the public in respect of privacy about the fact that it had provided other companies with NTT DoCoMo's mobile phone users' GPS location data, although specific individuals could not be identified by the data because the raw data had been statistically processed.

Japanese government considered (i) one of the causes of such social phenomenon (criticism by the public) was that APPI was partly unclear on the rules of the usage of personal data, (ii) but it was necessary to promote proper utilization of personal data while protecting data privacy, and therefore, (iii) it was necessary to clarify the rules.

As a result, under the amended APPI enforced in 2017, the definition of personal information was revised to be more specific, and provisions were added concerning the API.

In Japan, it is expected that the utilization of diverse and vast amounts of data including personal data (i.e. big data) will create innovation and new businesses. However, APPI requires, as a general rule, consent from data subjects to use their personal data for purposes other than those specified or to provide them to third parties. APPI, by its amendment, has added provisions under which the business operator may use and provide to third parties the API without obtaining the data subject's consent. This is expected to develop and foster new business or innovation.

This is an approach different from that on the "pseudonymization" under GDPR (further discussed later).

3. **Business Operator's Obligations**

(1). **Obligations of the Producer of Anonymously Processed Information**

The business operator who produces the API (limited to those constituting a database, the same applies hereafter) shall perform the following matters (36):

(a) to process personal information in accordance with the standards prescribed in the Rules so as to make it impossible to identify the data subject and restore the personal information;
(b) to ensure the security of the deleted information and the processing methods in accordance with the standards prescribed in the Rules;
(c) to disclose to the public the items contained in the API (e.g., ages, shopping behavior, travel habits, etc.) after the processing;
(a) not to collate the API with other information to identify the data subject;
(b) to take necessary measures to handle the API properly, including the security thereof and proper handling of complaints, and to endeavor to disclose these measures to the public; and
(c) before providing the API to a third party, in accordance with the Rules, (i) to disclose to the public the items contained in the API and provided to the third party and the method of the provision, and (ii) to clearly notify the third party that the information is the API;

The standards prescribed in the Rules (19) for the process includes:

(a) to delete all or part of the description contained in the personal information by which a specific individual can be identified or the individual identification codes as a whole, or replace them with other descriptions;
(b) to delete the codes which can link the original personal data and the resulting API or replace it with other codes (*1); and
(c) to delete unique descriptions (*2) or replace them with other descriptions.

(*1) e.g. management IDs to link the name of a user and his or her purchase history (API Report p51. 52 - the page numbers are those of the version with English translation, hereinafter the same)

(*2) e.g. a medical history of a rare disease, a record of the age of 116 years old (API Report p.55)

The standards prescribed in the Rules (20) for the security of the deleted information and the processing methods (collectively, the "processing methods etc.") include:
(a) to specify the responsibility of those who handle the processing methods etc.;
(b) to prepare, implement, evaluate and improve policy and procedures to properly handle the processing methods etc.; and
(c) to take necessary measures to prevent unauthorized access to the processing methods etc.

(2). Obligations of the Business Operator Other Than the Producer

The business operator other than the producer of the API (i.e. the business operator who obtained the API from the outside) shall perform the following matters:
(a) not to obtain the deleted information or the information on the method of processing or collate the API with other information to identify the data subject (38);
(b) to take necessary measures to handle the API properly, including the security thereof and proper handling of complaints, and to endeavor to disclose the measures to the public (39); and
(c) before providing the API to a third party, in accordance with the Rules, (i) to disclose to the public the items contained in the API and the method of the provision to a third party, and (ii) to clearly notify the third party that the information is API (37).

(3). Obligations Not Imposed Concerning Anonymously Processed Information

With respect to the API, the business operator is not subject to the obligations or restrictions of the following:
(a) specification of the purpose of use (15(1)) (the numbers here are those of the articles of APPI that apply to personal information or personal data);
(b) use beyond the purpose of use (15(2),16);
(c) notice to the data subject or disclosure to the public of the purpose of use (18);
(d) accuracy and deletion (19);
(e) provision to a third party in Japan (23) or in a foreign country (24);
(f) record keeping of the provision to a third party (25);
(g) confirmation and record keeping at the time of receipt from a third party (26); and
(h) disclosure, correction, addition or deletion, discontinuance of the use or deletion, or discontinuance of the provision to a third party, at the request of the data subject (29-30).

According to API Report (p.31-), the reason why these obligations or restrictions are not imposed is that the API is no longer personal data as the API cannot be "readily collated with other information" due to the prohibition of the collation of the API with other information to identify the data subject (36(5)).

4. **Guidelines on Anonymously Processed Information**

API Report and API GL explains in detail the processing methods to produce anonymously processed information and the handling thereof.

5. **Comparison with "Pseudonymization" in GDPR**

(1). "Anonymously Processed Information" in APPI

As mentioned above, in APPI, the term "anonymously processed information" is defined as the information that can be produced from processing personal information so as neither to be able to identify a specific individual nor to be able to restore the personal information, by deleting or replacing a part of descriptions in the said personal information (2(9)). The business operator who produces anonymously processed information shall ensure the security of <u>deleted information and the processing methods</u> (36(2)). That means the producer may keep the deleted information and processing methods.

In GDPR (4(9)), the term "pseudonymization" is defined as the processing of personal data in such a manner that the personal data can no longer be attributed to a specific data subject without the use of <u>additional information</u>, provided that such additional information is kept separately and is subject to technical and organizational measures to ensure that the personal data are not attributed to an identified or identifiable natural person.

Therefore, the "deleted information and processing methods" in APPI would be substantially same as the "additional information" in GDPR and the "anonymously processed information" in APPI would be substantially same as the personal data which have undergone "pseudonymization" in GDPR.

However, in the preamble 26 of GDPR, it is stated: "Personal data which have undergone pseudonymization, which could be attributed to a natural person by the use of additional information should be considered to be information on an identifiable natural person." Therefore, the personal data which have undergone pseudonymization still can be subject to the provisions in GDPR as personal data. In contrast, it is deemed under APPI that the "anonymously processed information" is no longer personal data because it is prohibited under APPI (36(5)) to collate the API with other information to identify the data subject and is subject to only the limited provisions as mentioned in 3, (1) and (2) above.

In GDPR, "pseudonymization" is regarded as one of appropriate technical and organizational measures to ensure the security (32(1)) or appropriate safeguards (6(4)(e)). In APPI, the processing to produce anonymously processed information is regarded as a way to utilize personal information.

These differences represent the difference in the basic stances of GDPR and APPI, while the personal data which have undergone "pseudonymization" and "anonymously processed information" are substantially the same.

(2). "Statistical Information" in APPI

In the API Report (p.23, 24), it is stated "The statistical information is the data obtained as the result of extracting certain items from personal information of many people and aggregating and classifying the items which are common to a certain group of people to understand quantitatively the trends or characteristics of the group. Therefore, as far as the correlation with specific individuals is excluded, the statistical information does not fall under the personal information in APPI and therefore is not subject to APPI."

In the preamble 26 of GDPR, it is stated "The principles of data protection should therefore not apply to anonymous information, namely information which does not relate to an identified or identifiable natural person or to personal data rendered anonymous in such a manner that the data subject is not or no longer identifiable. This Regulation does not, therefore, concern the processing of such anonymous information, including for statistical or research purposes."

Accordingly, the "statistical information" which is not subject to APPI is similar to or would be a type of the "anonymous information" in GDPR as they both have no correlation with a specific person.

XXIV. Protection of Individual Numbers

1. An Overview

The Individual Number (so-called "My Number") is a 12-digit number assigned to every Japanese citizen or every resident of Japan falling under certain conditions under the

"Act on the Use of Numbers to Identify a Specific Individual in Administrative Procedures" (the "Number Act") to streamline administrative operations in the field of social security, tax, and disaster countermeasures. The use of the Individual Numbers started from January 2016.

The Individual Number falls under the personal information defined in APPI. However, with respect to the introduction of the Individual Number system, there were worries or concerns on centralized management of personal information by the government; unauthorized monitoring, matching, use, or modification of information containing the Individual Numbers (the "Specific Personal Information"); and possible damage to individuals that might be caused by the foregoing.

As a result, for the handling of the Specific Personal Information by central government organizations, local governments, independent administrative agencies, etc. and private business operators (the "business operators"), the Number Act was enacted to stipulate restrictions stricter than APPI. The business operators are authorized to handle the Individual Numbers only for limited operations such as withholding tax from an employee's salary and social insurance-related procedures and are subject to the Number Act mainly in relation to these operations. However, except in certain cases, the business operator is also subject to the provisions of APPI with respect to the Specific Personal Information.

2. **Restriction of Collection**

Under APPI, the business operator shall specify the purpose of use of personal information (including the Individual Number) as specifically as possible (15) and may use it only within the scope of the specified purpose of use (16). However, APPI does not restrict the scope of the business for which the business operator may use personal information.

The Number Act limits the scope of use of the Individual Number only to specific administrative processes related to social security, taxation, and disaster management, including

the processes in the following situations (the "Process(es)") (9(3), Appendix 1).
(a) The business operator receives the Individual Numbers from its employees and writes them down on the documents relating to withholding tax from their salaries, salary payment reports, health insurance or employee pensions, and submits these documents to the tax office, local governments, Japan Pension Service, etc.
(b) A financial institution receives the Individual Numbers from its customers, writes them down in the payment records of dividends, etc., and submits them to the tax office.

The business operator may not request its employees to provide their Individual Numbers unless it is necessary for the Processes (14, 15).

The business operator, when obtaining an Individual Number, shall conduct the identity verification by prescribed procedures (16).

3. Restriction of Use

As mentioned above, the Number Act limits the scope of use of the Individual Numbers only for the Processes. Therefore, for example, the business operator may not use the Individual Numbers for general management of employees.

The Number Act also limits the case where the business operator may use the Specific Personal Information beyond its original purpose of use only to any of the following cases (30 (3)):
(a) When such use is necessary for a financial institution to pay money in the event of a particularly serious earthquake, weather, or other disasters which are specified by laws.
(b) When such use is necessary for the protection of the life, body or property of a person, and the consent of the data subject has been obtained or it is difficult to obtain the consent.

Furthermore, the business operator may create files such as databases of the Specific Personal Information only to the extent necessary for performing the Processes, and it shall not create the file in any other case (29).

4. Restriction of Provision to a Third Party

Under APPI, the business operator may provide personal information to a third party by obtaining the data subject's prior consent (23).

However, the business operator may not provide the Specific Personal Information to a third party (including an affiliated company) even with the data subject's consent (19), except in the limited cases specified in Article 19 of the Number Act (e.g. provision for the Processes).

Except in these cases, no one may request others to provide the Individual Numbers (15) or collect or store the Specific Personal Information (20).

5. Security of Handling

As stipulated in APPI, the business operator shall take necessary and appropriate security measures to prevent possible leakage or loss of or damage to the Specific Personal Information (20).

The "Secure Management Measures for the Specific Personal Information" attached to the "Guidelines on Proper Handling of the Specific Personal Information (For Business Operators)[10]" published by PPC are stricter than the measures recommended for other personal information in the General GL.

As stipulated in APPI, the business operator shall, in order to ensure the security of the Specific Personal Information, exercise necessary and appropriate supervision over:

---

[10] Guidelines on Proper Handling of Specific Personal Information (for Business Operators) (in Japanese language only)
https://www.ppc.go.jp/files/pdf/my_number_guideline_jigyosha.pdf

(a) the employee when having him or her handle the Specific Personal Information (21); and
(b) a third party when entrusting it with the handling thereof (22).

Although subcontracting is not prohibited under the Japanese Civil Code and APPI, the Number Act prohibits the entrusted third party from subcontracting the handling of the Processes without the business operator's prior approval (10 (1)).

XXV. Restriction of Advertisements by E-mails

The Act on Specified Commercial Transactions[11] ("ASCT") restricts advertisements by e-mail ("E-mail Advertisements") about specific types of sale or offer of goods or services to consumers (e.g., online sale) (12-3).

Under ASCT, the following obligations are imposed on business operators:
(a) The business operator shall not send E-mail Advertisements to a consumer unless he or she has requested or accepted to receive them in advance, with a few exceptions; and
(b) If the consumer rejected to receive the E-mail Advertisements after the request or acceptance, the business operator shall discontinue sending them.
(c) The business operator shall make and maintain the record of the request or acceptance for three years from sending the last E-mail Advertisement.
(d) The business operator shall display the information necessary for consumers to reject receiving the E-mail Advertisements (e.g. e-mail address, URL) in a manner that consumers can easily recognize the information.

---

[11] English Translation of the Act on Specified Commercial Transactions with its original text
http://www.japaneselawtranslation.go.jp/law/detail/?id=2065&vm=04&re=01

XXVI. Regulations on Cookies

In Japan, there is no law that directly regulates cookies. However, if it is easy to collate the information obtained by using cookies with other information (e.g. a user registration), and thereby a specific individual can be identified, APPI applies to the information so obtained.

XXVII. Sample Agreements for the Provision of Personal Data to a Third Party in a Foreign Country

There are two types of SCC under EU Data Protection Directive for the transfer of personal data from an entity in EEA (the data exporter) to an entity outside EEA (the data importer). They are:
(a) the SCC in which the data importer is a controller; and
(b) the SCC in which the data importer is a processor

As mentioned in XX-2, with respect to the provision of personal data from the business operator in Japan (the data exporter) to a third party in a foreign country (the data importer), if it is ensured by a contract etc. between them that the data importer shall continuously take the measures equivalent to those which the data exporter (or a business operator) should take under APPI, such provision may be made without the data subject's prior consent (24, Rules 11). Such contract is, so to say, a Japanese version of SCC.

The following are the drafts prepared by the author of this book of Japanese versions of SCC for the provision of personal data from the business operator in Japan (the data exporter) to a third party in a foreign country (the data importer):
(i) "PERSONAL DATA PROVISION AGREEMENT", in which the data importer uses the personal data for itself. This corresponds to SCC (a) above. – Agreement (i).
(ii) "AGREEMENT FOR ENTRUSTMENT OF HANDLING

OF PERSONAL DATA", in which the data importer handles the personal data on behalf of the data exporter. This corresponds to SCC (b) above. — Agreement (ii).

The Agreement (i) could be used in the following cases by modifying it according to the specific situation in each case:

- A company in Japan provides the personal data of its employees to its parent company in a foreign country for human resources management by the parent company;
- A company in Japan provides the personal data of its Japanese consumers to its parent company in a foreign country for the parent company's business;
- A parent company in Japan provides to its subsidiary in a foreign country the personal data of the parent company's employee who will be dispatched to the subsidiary;
- The member hotels of an international hotel chain exchange and jointly use the personal data of their respective guests; or
- A group of companies establishes an intranet site on which the same departments (e.g. finance) of the group companies in different countries (including Japan) introduce their respective department members.

The Agreement (ii) could be used in the following cases by modifying it according to the specific situation in each case:

- A company in Japan entrusts the entry work of its customers' data to its subsidiary in a foreign country; or
- A company in Japan entrusts the analysis of big data containing personal data to a third party in a foreign country.

1. PERSONAL DATA PROVISION AGREEMENT

This Personal Data Provision Agreement (this "Agreement") is made and entered into as of the [ ] day of [ ], 20[ ] ("Effective Date") by [ ], a corporation duly organized and existing under the laws of Japan, having its principal offices at [ ], Japan ("Data Exporter") and [ ], a corporation duly organized and existing under the laws of [ ], having its principal offices at [ ], [Name of a foreign country:] ("Data Importer").

WHEREAS, the parties to this Agreement (collectively the "Parties" and respectively the "Party") desire provision of personal data from Data Exporter to Data Importer; and

WHEREAS, the Parties desire to do this provision of the personal data by executing a written agreement that ensures Data Importer shall continuously take the measures equivalent to those which Data Exporter should take with respect to the handling of personal data under Article 24 (Restriction on Provision to a Third Party in a Foreign Country) of the Japanese Act on the Protection of Personal Information ("APPI").

NOW, THEREFORE, the Parties agree as follows:

ARTICLE 1. DEFINITIONS

In addition to terms elsewhere defined in this Agreement, the following terms shall have the meanings set forth in this Article 1 for the purposes of this Agreement:
(a) The term "Personal Data" means the information described in Exhibit A attached hereto ("Exhibit A").
(b) The term "Data Subject" means the specific individual who can be identified by the Personal Data.

ARTICLE 2.   PROVISION OF PERSONAL DATA

1. Data Exporter shall provide Data Importer with the Personal Data in accordance with Exhibit A, and Data Importer shall receive and use and otherwise handle them in accordance with this Agreement.
2. If Exhibit A includes the provision regarding the term of this Agreement (the "Term"), the Personal Data shall be provided to and may be used or otherwise handled by Data Importer only during the Term.

< Explanation >

Exhibit A could include the form or method (e.g., delivery of recording media, download from Data Exporter's website), place, and time or deadline of the provision of the Personal Data and conditions for acceptance.

As mentioned in XIII-5(4), under APPI, the business operator is required to make a record of certain items (i) when provided personal data to a third party (in Japan or a foreign country) (25) or (ii) when receiving personal data from a third party (in Japan or a foreign country) (26), but in the case where such items are stated in a written agreement executed for the provision of the personal data, the business operator may use the agreement as the record (Rule 12(3), 16(3))). Considering it, Exhibit A should also include the following items:
(a) the information by which the data subject can be identified (e.g. the category of the data subjects)
(b) the items of the personal data (e.g. a name, address, telephone number, age, purchase history);
(c) the circumstances under which Data Exporter collected the personal data (e.g. from whom and how to);
(d) The prerequisite basis of the provision of personal data (See XX-2, Foreign GL p.3,4):
   (i) if it is the data subject's consent to the provision of his or her personal data to third parties in general (i.e. without specifically referring to a third party in a foreign country) under Article 23 (1) of APPI (the

"general consent"), that such general consent has been obtained;
(ii) if it is the opt-out mechanism under Article 23 (2) of APPI for personal data including the Personal Data, that PPC had published the information relating to the items to be reported by Data Exporter; or
(iii) if it is the joint-use of the personal data under Article 23 (5)-3 of APPI, that Data Exporter has notified the Data Subject of the items stipulated in Article 23 (5)-3 that cover the provision of the Personal Data to Data Importer for the Purpose of Use or has made them easily accessible to the Data Subject.

The provision of the Personal Data may be made (i) only once, or, (ii) repeatedly during a certain period of time or (iii) in a form of license with a limited license period. Paragraph 2 of this Article 1 is for the case (ii) or (iii).

ARTICLE 3. REPRESENTATIONS AND WARRANTIES

1. Data Exporter represents and warrants:
   (a) that Data Exporter has collected the Personal Data lawfully and properly in compliance with APPI and the circumstances under which Data Exporter collected the Personal Data are as described in Exhibit A; and
   (b) that Data Exporter has complied and will comply with APPI with respect to the provision of the Personal Data to Data Importer.
2. Data Importer represents and warrants:
   (a) that Data Importer has established and is maintaining the system to take necessary and appropriate security measures to prevent possible leakage or loss of, or damage to, the Personal Data; and
   (b) that Data Importer has no reason to believe, at the time of the execution of this Agreement, in the existence of any law that would have a substantial adverse effect on the performance of its obligations under this Agreement.

< Explanation >

- Article 3, Paragraph 1

This paragraph is included considering the following:
(i) SCC Set II under EU Data Protection Directive stipulates "The data exporter warrants and undertakes that...(the) personal data have been collected, processed and transferred in accordance with the laws applicable to the data exporter" (I-a).
(ii) Under APPI, the business operator shall not collect personal information by deception or other wrongful means (17(1)).
(iii) Under APPI, the business operator, when receiving personal data from a third party, shall confirm certain items including the circumstances under which the third party collected the personal data (26(1), (3)).
(iv) Under APPI, the business operator shall not handle the personal information beyond the scope necessary to achieve the purpose of use without obtaining the data subject's prior consent (16(1), (3)). Therefore, when the business operator provides personal data to a third party, the provision to the third party for the third party's own purpose of use must be included in the purpose of use which the business operator has disclosed under APPI (27, 18(1) or 18(2)). If not, it constitutes a violation of APPI.

- Article 3, Paragraph 2, (a)

The Data Importer's representations and warranties in (a) are not directly required by APPI. However, as a prerequisite to use this Agreement as the "adequate and reasonable means" (by which obtaining the Data Subject's consent is exempted), Data Exporter should confirm, before and at the time of the execution of this Agreement, that Data Importer has already established and is maintaining the system to take necessary and appropriate measures to ensure the secure management of the Personal Data.

- Article 3, Paragraph 2, (b)

This provision follows II-c of SCC Set II. For example, if the government of the country in which Data Importer is established has the authority to collect the Personal Data from Data Importer unconditionally (e.g. for any public security purpose), it would be difficult to keep the level of protection equivalent to that of APPI in that country.

ARTICLE 4. MEASURES EQUIVALENT TO THOSE REQUIRED BY APPI

1. Data Importer shall use the Personal Data for the purpose described in Exhibit A (the "Purpose of Use").
2. Data Importer shall not handle the Personal Data beyond the scope necessary to achieve the Purpose of Use, without obtaining the Data Subject's prior consent.
3. Data Importer shall not change the Purpose of Use beyond the scope reasonably relevant to the Purpose of Use before the change, without obtaining the Data Subject's prior consent.
4. When Data Importer has changed the Purpose of Use to any purpose other than the purpose described in Exhibit A, it shall notify the Data Subject of the purpose or disclose it to the public in Japan.
5. Data Importer shall endeavor to keep the Personal Data accurate and up-to-date, to the extent necessary to achieve the Purpose of Use and delete the Personal Data without delay after its use became no longer necessary.
6. Data Importer shall take and maintain necessary and appropriate security measures to prevent possible leakage or loss of, or damage to, the Personal Data, taking due consideration of the guidelines or other recommendations of the Personal Information Protection Commission, Japan.
7. Data Importer, when having its employees handle the Personal Data, shall exercise necessary and appropriate supervision over them to ensure the security of the

Personal Data as provided in paragraph 6 above.
8. Data Importer, when entrusting a third party with all or any part of the handling of the Personal Data, shall exercise necessary and appropriate supervision over the third party to ensure the security of the Personal Data at the level of security equivalent to or higher than that of Data Importer provided in paragraph 6 above.
9. Data Importer shall not provide the Personal Data to a third party in Japan without obtaining the Data Subject's prior consent.
10. Data Importer shall, when providing the Personal Data to a third party in a country other than Japan, obtain the Data Subject's prior consent that specifically refers to the provision to a third party in any of the countries including that country.
11. When Data Importer provided the Personal Data to any third party in or outside Japan, it shall make a record of the date of the provision, the name of the third party (or other information by which the third party can be identified, or if the personal data were provided to unspecified third parties, that fact), and other information required under APPI and keep the record for three (3) years or more from the date of the provision.
12. Data Importer shall, before starting the use of the Personal Data, disclose to the public in Japan the following information:
    (a) the name of Data Importer;
    (b) the Purpose of Use;
    (c) the procedures and ways of the request of the Data Subject under paragraphs 13 through 17 of this Article and of the response by Data Importer to that request under APPI; and
    (d) the contact information for the Data Subject to lodge a complaint with Data Importer concerning its handling of the Personal Data.
13. If so requested by the Data Subject, Data Importer shall notify the Data Subject of the Purpose of Use without delay.
14. If so requested by the Data Subject, Data Importer shall disclose the Personal Data to the Data Subject without

delay.
15. If the Personal Data is not accurate and Data Importer is requested by the Data Subject for correction, addition or deletion, Data Importer shall undertake investigations without delay, and, based on the result, make the correction, addition or deletion, to the extent it is necessary to achieve the Purpose of Use.
16. If Data Importer handled the Personal Data beyond the scope necessary to achieve the Purpose of Use without the Data Subject's prior consent, Data Importer, even if not so requested by the Data Subject, shall discontinue the use of or delete the Personal Data immediately.
17. If Data Importer provided the Personal Data to any third party in or outside Japan without obtaining necessary Data Subject's prior consent, Data Importer, even if not so requested by the Data Subject, shall discontinue the provision immediately.
18. Data Importer shall establish and maintain the system necessary to handle appropriately and promptly the Data Subjects' complaints about the handling of their Personal Data.
19. If so provided in Exhibit B attached hereto ("Exhibit B"), Data Importer may and shall entrust Data Exporter with (i) the performance of a part of the obligations set forth in paragraphs 12, 13, and 14, and/or (ii) a part of the communication with or response to the Data Subject necessary to perform the obligations set forth in paragraphs 15 through 18, and Data Exporter shall perform the entrusted matters on behalf of Data Importer, in accordance with the terms and conditions set forth in Exhibit B.

< Explanation >

What kind of provisions should be included in the written agreement to ensure that Data Importer shall continuously take the measures equivalent to those which Data Exporter should take with respect to the handling of the personal data under APPI? According to Foreign GL (p. 9), the agreement needs not necessarily include all the provisions of APPI on the business operator 's obligations. Rather, if it includes all the provisions including their conditions and exceptions, it will be too complex for Data Importer and its employees to understand.

In contrast, only generally stipulating that Data Importer should comply with (i) APPI, (ii) the data protection laws of Data Importer 's country that ensure the level of data protection equivalent to or higher than APPI, or (iii) OECD guidelines or APEC Cross Border Privacy Rules (CBPR), would not be sufficient (See PPC's stance on the public opinions regarding draft Foreign GL; 750, 752, 765).

In addition, for example, if the personal data were leaked from Data Importer, Data Exporter would need to prove it had complied with APPI in providing the Personal Data to Data Importer. Therefore, it will be desirable to stipulate specifically to some extent Data Importer's obligations.

Considering the above, this Agreement restates the business operator's obligations under APPI simplified by removing most exceptions and minor conditions or making the obligations stricter than those under APPI.

If so provided in Exhibit B, Data Importer may entrust Data Exporter with the performance of a part of the obligations or communication with the Data Subjects set forth in paragraphs 12 through 18 (e.g. disclosure at the request by the Data Subject), as such entrustment is allowable (Foreign GL p.24-32) and would be practically necessary in many cases. Paragraph 19 is for that purpose.

To the following Articles of APPI, the paragraphs of this Article 4 correspond as follows.

APPI Article 15 (Specification of the purpose of use) - Paragraph 1, 2
APPI Article 16 (Restriction concerning the purpose of use [Purpose limitation]) - Paragraph 3
APPI Article 18(1) (Notification or disclosure to the public of the purpose of use after the collection) - Paragraphs 12 and 13
APPI Article 18 (3) (Notification of the change of purpose of use) - Paragraph 4

APPI Article 19 (Accuracy of the personal data etc.) - Paragraph 5
APPI Article 20 (Security of Handling) - Paragraph 6
APPI Article 21 (Supervision over employees) - Paragraph 7
APPI Article 22 (Supervision over a third party to whom the handling of the personal data was entrusted) - Paragraph 8
APPI Article 23 (Restriction of the provision to a third party in Japan) - Paragraph 9
APPI Article 24 (Restriction of the provision to a third party in a foreign country) - Paragraph 10
APPI Article 25 (Record keeping on the provision to a third party) - Paragraph 11
APPI Article 27 (Publication about the retained personal data) - Paragraphs 12 and 13
APPI Article 28 (Right of data subjects: Disclosure) - Paragraph 14
APPI Article 29 (Right of data subjects: Correction etc.) - Paragraph 15
APPI Article 30 (Right of data subjects: Discontinuance of use or deletion or discontinuance of the provision to a third party) – Paragraphs 16 and 17
APPI Article 35 (Handling of complaints) - Paragraph 18

ARTICLE 5. FEES AND PAYMENTS

As consideration for the provision of the Personal Data hereunder, Data Importer shall pay Data Exporter fee(s) in accordance with Exhibit C attached to this Agreement.

< Explanation >
If no fee is paid, this Article should be deleted.

ARTICLE 6. AMENDMENT TO APPI

If APPI is amended after the execution of this Agreement and any obligation of the business operator under APPI is added or changed to become stricter than the obligations of Data Importer under Article 4, Article 4 shall be deemed to have been amended to reflect the addition or change. Data Importer shall, at its sole responsibility and in a timely manner, obtain the information about any the addition or change of APPI.

< Explanation >

As mentioned above, it should be ensured by this Agreement that Data Importer shall <u>continuously</u> take the measures equivalent to (or stricter than) those which the business operator should take under APPI. That means Data Importer's obligations under this Agreement should be adapted to a possible amendment to APPI in the future. This paragraph deals with this issue.

ARTICLE 7.   TERMINATION

1. If Data Importer fails to comply with any provision of this Agreement and the failure has not been cured within [ ] after the receipt of a written notice from Data Exporter, Data Exporter may terminate this Agreement immediately by giving a written notice to Data Importer.
2. If Data Importer files a petition in bankruptcy or a petition in bankruptcy is filed against it, or if it becomes insolvent or bankrupt, makes a general assignment for the benefit of creditors, or goes into liquidation or receivership, Data Exporter may terminate this Agreement immediately by giving a written notice to Data Importer.

< Explanation >

If the provision of the Personal Data is made only once, and no substantial transaction or communication between Data Exporter and Data Importer thereafter is intended, it would be necessary to modify this Article so that this Agreement terminates automatically without any notice from Data Exporter when one of the above-mentioned causes occurs.

ARTICLE 8.   EFFECTS OF TERMINATION OR EXPIRATION

1. Upon termination or expiration of this Agreement, Data Importer shall immediately (a) discontinue any handling of any Personal Data and (b) return or delete all the Personal Data according to Data Exporter's instruction, and (c) provide Data Exporter with a writing that an authorized representative of Data Importer certifies all the Personal Data were returned or destroyed. Data Exporter shall have the right, at its own expense, on reasonable prior written notice, to inspect any record or information or facility to verify that all the Personal Data were returned or destroyed, or to have a third party conduct such inspection. Such inspection shall be conducted during reasonable business hours at the location where such record or information or the Personal Data may be stored.
2. The termination or expiration of this Agreement at any time, in any circumstances and for whatever reason does not exempt Data Importer from the obligations and/or conditions under this Agreement as regards the handling of the Personal Data provided to Data Importer.
3. In addition to paragraph 2 above, those provisions that by their nature should survive termination or expiration of this Agreement, will survive termination or expiration of this Agreement.

<Explanation>
Paragraph 1 of this Article 8 was made referring to the "Extra termination clause" in "ILLUSTRATIVE COMMERCIAL CLAUSES (OPTIONAL)" of SCC Set II.

Paragraph 2 of this Article 8 was made referring to VI-(d) of SCC Set II.

ARTICLE 9.   DISCLAIMER OF WARRANTY

1. **EXCEPT AS EXPRESSLY PROVIDED IN THIS**

AGREEMENT, TO THE MAXIMUM EXTENT PERMITTED BY APPLICABLE LAW, THE PERSONAL DATA ARE PROVIDED "AS IS" AND WITHOUT WARRANTIES OR CONDITIONS OF ANY KIND, INCLUDING BUT NOT LIMITED TO ANY IMPLIED WARRANTIES AND CONDITIONS OF MERCHANTABILITY AND FITNESS FOR A PARTICULAR PURPOSE.
2. DATA EXPORTER MAKES NO WARRANTIES, INCLUDING, BUT NOT LIMITED TO ANY WARRANTY REGARDING ACCURACY AND INTEGRITY, EITHER EXPRESS OR IMPLIED, STATUTORY OR OTHERWISE, WITH RESPECT TO ANY INFORMATION THAT DATA EXPORTER HAS PROVIDED, OR MAY PROVIDE TO DATA IMPORTER IN RELATION TO APPI.

< Explanation >

I-C of SCC Set II stipulates that the data exporter "will provide the Data Importer, when so requested, with copies of relevant data protection laws or references to them (where relevant, and not including legal advice) of the country in which the data exporter is established."   Under Paragraph 2 of this Article 9, Data Exporter may, but is not obliged to, provide Data Importer with information about APPI including its English translation, and rather excludes any warranty about such information, as, for example, it is too difficult to make a complete English translation of APPI.

ARTICLE 10.   LIABILITY AND INDEMNIFICATION

1. Each Party shall be liable to the other Party for damages, cost, charge, expense or loss ("Damages") it causes by any breach of any provision of this Agreement or any law concerning personal data protection or privacy including APPI that applies to the Party ("Breach"). Liability as between the Parties is limited to actual damage suffered. Punitive damages (i.e. damages intended to punish a party for its outrageous conduct) are specifically

excluded. Each Party shall be liable to the Data Subjects for damages it causes by any Breach.
2. Each Party (the "Indemnifying Party") shall defend, indemnify and hold the other Party (the "Indemnified Party") harmless from any Damages arising from or in connection with any actual or threatened claim, demand, or investigation by a third party (including a competent authority) (each a "Claim") to the extent such Claim is based on or arises from or relates to any Breach by the Indemnifying Party. Indemnification hereunder is contingent upon:
   (i) the Indemnified Party promptly notifying the Indemnifying Party of the Claim;
   (ii) the Indemnifying Party having sole control of the defense and settlement of the Claim; and
   (iii) the Indemnified Party providing reasonable cooperation and assistance to the Indemnifying Party in defense of the Claim.

< Explanation >

Article 10, Paragraph 1 was made referring to III (a) of SCC Set II.
Article 10, Paragraph 2 was made referring to the provision "Indemnification between the data exporter and data importer" in "ILLUSTRATIVE COMMERCIAL CLAUSES (OPTIONAL)" of SCC Set II.

ARTICLE 11.   MISCELLANEOUS

1. This Agreement (including exhibits constituting a part of this Agreement) constitutes the entire agreement between the Parties with respect to the subject matter hereof and supersedes all prior agreements, understandings and negotiations, both written and oral, between the Parties with respect to the subject matter hereof. No modification of this Agreement shall be binding unless executed in writing by both Parties.
2. This Agreement may not be assigned or transferred by either Party without the express prior written consent of

the other Party.
3. The waiver by each Party of a breach of any provision contained herein shall be in writing and shall in no way be construed as a waiver of any subsequent breach of such provision or the waiver of the provision itself.
4. Except as otherwise expressly provided in this Agreement, nothing contained in this Agreement shall be construed as creating a partnership, joint venture or agency relationship between the Parties or as granting either Party the authority to bind or contract in the name of or on the account of the other Party or to make any statements, representations, warranties or commitments on behalf of the other Party.
5. If any provision of this Agreement shall be invalid or unenforceable, such invalidity or unenforceability shall not render the entire Agreement invalid. Rather, this Agreement shall be construed as if not containing the particular invalid or unenforceable provision, and the rights and obligations of each Party shall be construed and enforced accordingly.
6. Any notice, consent or other communication required or permitted to be given in writing hereunder ("Notice") shall be (a) mailed by registered or certified mail, postage prepaid with return receipt requested, (b) sent by internationally recognized courier service (such as FedEx or DHL) which provides a delivery receipt, (c) delivered in person, or (d) sent by facsimile or electronic mail (with the sender's confirmation letter thereof sent by the registered or certified mail or the courier service), to the address specified below or to such changed address as may be specified by a like Notice from one Party to the other Party. If the Notice is mailed by registered or certified mail or sent by courier service, it shall be deemed to have been given [   ] business days after the mailing or sending. If the Notice is delivered in person or sent by facsimile or electronic mail, it shall be deemed to have been given upon receipt.

If to Data Exporter:
Name: [   ]

Address: [   ]
Attention: [   ]
Facsimile number: [   ]
Electronic mail address: [   ]

If to Data Importer:
Name: [   ]
Address: [   ]
Attention: [   ]
Facsimile number: [   ]
Electronic mail address: [   ]

7. This Agreement shall be construed in accordance with and governed by the laws of Japan without reference to principles of conflict of laws.
8. Any dispute arising out of or in connection with this Agreement, including any question regarding its existence, validity or termination, shall be referred to and finally resolved by arbitration administered by [   ] in accordance with [   ]. The seat of the arbitration shall be [   ]. The language of the arbitration shall be English.

IN WITNESS WHEREOF, the Parties have caused this Agreement to be executed by their duly authorized representatives as of the Effective Date.

Data Exporter

Company Name: [   ]

By: [   ]

Printed Name: [   ]

Title: [   ]

Data Importer

Company Name: [ ]

By: [   ]

Printed Name: [   ]

Title: [   ]

EXHIBIT A

1. **Descriptions of the Personal Data**

2. **The items of the Personal Data**
   (e.g. a name, address, telephone number, age, purchase history of the Data Subjects)

3. **The information by which the Data Subject can be identified**
   (e.g. the category of the Data Subjects)

4. **Delivery of the Personal Data**

   (An example) Within ten (10) days after both Parties have executed this Agreement, Data Exporter shall notify Data Importer of the URL of a website from which the Personal Data may be downloaded and an ID and password for the download. Data Importer may download the Personal Data from the website using the ID and password. The delivery of the Personal Data shall be deemed to have been completed by such notification.

5. **The circumstances under which Data Exporter collected the Personal Data**
   (e.g. from whom and how to)

   (An example) Data Exporter collected the Personal Data on its website. The Data Subjects who visited the site entered the Personal Data in the user registration form on the site. Before the Personal Data were transmitted to the server managed by Data Exporter, Data Exporter' privacy policy including Data Exporter' purpose of use of the Personal Data had been displayed to the Data Subjects, and the Data Subjects pressed a button on the site to agree to the policy.

6. **The prerequisite basis of the provision of the Personal Data**
   (Place a check mark in the square bracket of the corresponding item)

   [   ] It is the Data Subject's consent to the provision of his or her personal data to third parties in general (i.e. without specifically referring to a third party in a foreign country) under Article 23 (1) of APPI.
   [   ] Such general consent has been obtained.

   [   ] It is the opt-out mechanism under Article 23 (2) of APPI for personal data including the Personal Data.
   [   ] The Personal Information Protection Commission, Japan had published the information relating to the items to be reported by Data Exporter.

   [   ] It is the joint-use of the Personal Data under Article 23 (5)-3 of APPI.
   [   ] Data Exporter has notified the Data Subject of the items stipulated in Article 23 (5)-3 that cover the provision of the Personal Data to Data Importer for the Purpose of Use, or has made the items easily accessible to the Data Subject.

7. **The Purpose of Use**
   (Specify it as specific as possible)

8. **The term of this Agreement (if any)**

   (An example) This Agreement shall come into force on the Effective Date, and, unless sooner terminated, shall continue in full force and effect for one (1) year from the Effective Date. Thereafter, this Agreement shall be automatically extended for successive periods of one (1) year each, unless either Party shall have otherwise notified to the other Party in writing at least [   ] prior to the expiry of this Agreement or any extension thereof.

EXHIBIT B

[If Data Importer, under paragraph 19 of Article 4, entrusts Data Exporter with (i) the performance of a part of the obligations set forth in paragraphs 12, 13, and 14 of Article 4, or (ii) a part of the communication with the Data Subject necessary to perform the obligations set forth in paragraphs 15 through 18 of Article 4, specify such entrusted obligations or communication, and the terms and conditions of the entrustment.]

EXHIBIT C

FEES AND PAYMENTS FOR THE PROVISION OF THE PERSONAL DATA

[If Data Importer pays Data Exporter fees as consideration for the provision of the Personal Data, specify below the fees and the payment conditions thereof.]

2. AGREEMENT FOR ENTRUSTMENT OF HANDLING OF PERSONAL DATA

This Agreement for Entrustment of Handling of Personal Data ("this Agreement") is made and entered into as of the [   ] day of [   ], ("Effective Date") by [   ], a corporation duly organized and existing under the laws of Japan, having its principal offices at [   ] , Japan ("Data Exporter") and [   ], a corporation duly organized and existing under the laws of [   ], having its principal offices at [   ], [Name of a foreign country:] ("Data Importer") .

WHEREAS, Data Exporter located in Japan desires to entrust Data Importer located in [Name of the foreign country:] with the handling of personal data, and for that purpose, to provide the personal data to Data Importer,

WHEREAS, Data Importer is willing to accept such entrustment and provision; and

WHEREAS, the parties to this Agreement (collectively the "Parties" and respectively the "Party") desire to do this provision of the personal data by executing a written agreement that ensures Data Importer shall continuously take the measures equivalent to those which Data Exporter should take with respect to handling of personal data under Article 24 (Restriction on Provision to a Third Party in a Foreign Country) of the Japanese Act on the Protection of Personal Information ("APPI").

NOW, THEREFORE, the Parties agree as follows:

ARTICLE 1.   DEFINITIONS

In addition to terms elsewhere defined in this Agreement, the following terms shall have the meanings set forth in this Article 1 for purposes of this Agreement:

(a) The term "Personal Data" means the information described in Exhibit A attached hereto ("Exhibit A").
(b) The term "Data Subject" means the specific individual that can be identified by the Personal Data.
(c) The terms "Purpose of Entrustment" and "Descriptions of Entrustment" mean the purpose and descriptions of the entrustment specified in Exhibit A respectively.
(d) The term "Secure Management Measures" means the measures specified in Exhibit B attached hereto ("Exhibit B") which Data Importer shall take in handling the Personal Data.

ARTICLE 2. REPRESENTATIONS AND WARRANTIES

1. Data Exporter represents and warrants that it has complied and will comply with APPI with respect to the entrustment of the handling and the provision of the Personal Data to Data Importer.
2. Data Importer represents and warrants:
    (a) that Data Importer has established and is maintaining the system necessary to take the Secure Management Measures; and
    (b) that Data Importer has no reason to believe, at the time of execution of this Agreement, in the existence of any law that would have a substantial adverse effect on the performance of its obligations under this Agreement.

ARTICLE 3. HANDLING OF PERSONAL DATA

1. The Data Importer shall handle the Personal Data in accordance with this Agreement.
2. The Data Importer shall handle the Personal Data for the Purpose of Entrustment and within the scope of the Descriptions of Entrustment and shall not handle the Personal Data for any other purpose or beyond the scope of the Descriptions of Entrustment.
3. Data Exporter may change the Purpose of Entrustment

and/or the scope of the Descriptions of Entrustment by a written agreement with Data Importer, provided, however, that if there is any legal obligation Data Exporter must fulfill to so change, such as obtaining the consent of or notification to the Data Subject, Data Exporter shall take appropriate actions accordingly.
4. Data Importer shall keep the Personal Data accurate and up-to-date, within the scope necessary to achieve the Purpose of Entrustment and delete the Personal Data without delay when their use is no longer required for the Purpose of Entrustment.
5. Data Importer shall take the Secure Management Measures.
6. Data Importer, when having its employees handle the Personal Data, shall exercise necessary and appropriate supervision over them to ensure the security of the Personal Data in accordance with the Secure Management Measures.
7. Data Importer shall not entrust any part of the handling of the Personal Data to any third party, without Data Exporter's express prior written consent.
8. If Data Importer entrusts any part of the handling of the Personal Data to a third party by obtaining Data Exporter's express prior written consent, it shall exercise necessary and appropriate supervision over the third party to ensure the security of the Personal Data in accordance with the Secure Management Measures.
9. In addition to the obligations provided in the paragraphs 7 and 8 of this Article, Data Importer shall not provide the Personal Data to any third party (regardless of whether the third party is located in or outside Japan), without Data Exporter's express prior written consent.
10. In the event Data Importer has its employees or a third party handle the Personal Data in accordance with paragraph 6 or 8 of this Article, Data Importer shall impose them the same obligations as Data Importer's obligations concerning the handling of the Personal Data hereunder by way of written contracts or legally binding rules and shall remain fully liable for their performance of such obligations.

11. Data Importer shall maintain in confidence the Personal Data during the term of this Agreement and even after the expiration or termination hereof, and shall not disclose the Personal Data to any other party without Data Exporter's express prior written consent, provided, however, that Data Importer may disclose the Personal Data only to its employees whom Data Importer authorizes to handle the Personal Data or the third party to whom Data Importer entrusts the handling of the Personal Data by obtaining Data Exporter's prior written consent, to the extent necessary for their respective duties.

ARTICLE 4   RECORD, REPORT, AND AUDIT

1. Data Importer shall make and maintain records of the information that Data Exporter designates regarding Data Importer's handling of the Personal Data ("Handling Records") in a manner instructed by Data Exporter until [ ] years have elapsed after the expiration or termination of this Agreement ("Record Keeping Period").
2. Data Exporter shall have the right to request Data Importer to report on the status of the handling of the Personal Data by Data Importer at any time during the Record Keeping Period. In response to that request, Data importer shall, promptly, submit the Handling Records, orally reply or explain, submit a certificate of the authorized representative of Data Importer, or otherwise respond, with respect to the status in accordance with instructions Data Exporter reasonably gives.
3. Data Exporter shall have the right, at its own expense, on reasonable prior written notice, to inspect and audit the Handling Records (including the database which contains them) and the actual handling of the Personal Data, during the Record Keeping Period, or to have a third party conduct such inspection and audit. Such inspection and audit shall be conducted during reasonable business hours at the location where Data Importer is maintaining the Handling Records and/or is handling the Personal Data.

ARTICLE 5   REQUEST FOR IMPROVEMENT OR CHANGE

1. In any of the following events, Data Exporter shall have the right to request Data Importer to make improvements or changes to the Secure Management Measures or the specific manners to implement them, and Data Importer shall promptly respond to it:
    (a) if Data Importer is not complying with any of the Secure Management Measures; or
    (b) if Data Exporter considers that it is necessary to make such improvements or changes.
2. In the event either Party anticipates that the cost of handling of the Personal Data by Data Importer will increase or decrease due to the improvements or changes mentioned in (b) of paragraph 1 above, that Party may request the other Party for consultation on the change of the fee provided in Article 9 with giving the specific reason for and the anticipated amount of, the increase or decrease, and the other Party shall respond to it in good faith. In the case of (a) of paragraph 1 above, Data Importer shall bear all the costs necessary for the improvements or changes.

ARTICLE 6   MEASURES TO BE TAKEN IN CASE OF UNAUTHORIZED DISCLOSURE, LOSS OR DAMAGE

1. If any unauthorized disclosure or loss of or damage to the Personal Data (the "Leakage, etc.") has occurred or is reasonably judged to have occurred, Data Importer shall immediately report it to Data Exporter.
2. In the case of paragraph 1 above, Data Importer shall cooperate with Data Exporter with respect to any one or more action(s) listed below or take such action(s) by itself, in accordance with Data Exporter's reasonable instructions:
    (a) Prevention of expansion of the Leakage, etc.,
    (b) Factual investigation and identification of the causes,

- (c) Identification of the extent of the impact,
- (d) Development and implementation of recurrence prevention measures,
- (e) Report to the Personal Information Protection Commission, Japan ("PPC"),
- (f) Notification to the Data Subject who may be affected, depending on the level of anticipated impact,
- (g) Publication of the facts and recurrence prevention measures, and/or
- (h) Other actions Data Exporter may reasonably request.

ARTICLE 7   DISCLOSURE REQUESTS FROM ADMINISTRATIVE OR JUDICIAL ORGANIZATIONS

1. If Data Importer was requested to disclose the Personal Data to an administrative or judicial organization or a third party entrusted thereby under the laws of the country in which Data Importer is established or any other applicable laws, Data Importer shall notify Data Exporter thereof and obtain its prior written consent to such disclosure, except when it is not permitted by such laws or not reasonably practicable to so notify or seek consent.
2. Even if Data Importer is unable to notify or seek prior consent in accordance with the paragraph 1 above, it shall take all the following measures to the extent permitted under the applicable laws and reasonably practicable:
   - (a) to ensure that Data Exporter may submit opinions, request the protective order for the Personal Data, or otherwise participate in the response to the disclosure request;
   - (b) to minimize the disclosure;
   - (c) to request the protective order for the Personal Data; and
   - (d) to notify Data Exporter of the disclosure as soon as practicably possible thereafter.

ARTICLE 8   AMENDMENT TO APPI

1. If it becomes necessary to amend this Agreement (including the Secure Management Measures) due to any amendment to APPI or guidelines published by PPC with respect to APPI, the Parties shall consult with each other in good faith and execute an amendment agreement to make necessary and reasonable changes to this Agreement.
2. If either Party anticipates that the cost of handling of the Personal Data by Data Importer will increase or decrease due to the amendment to APPI or the guidelines of PPC, the Party may request the other Party for consultation on the change of the fees provided in Article 9 with giving the specific reasons and the anticipated amount of, the increase or decrease, and the other Party shall respond to it in good faith.
3. If the Parties fail to reach an agreement to change the fee within [   ] from either Party's request for consultation under paragraph 2 above, each Party may terminate this Agreement with [   ] day prior written notice to the other Party.
4. If any law or its amendment applicable to Data Importer is likely to have a substantial adverse effect on the performance of its obligations under this Agreement, Data Importer shall immediately notify Data Exporter thereof in writing.
5. In the event of paragraph 4 above, the Parties shall consult with each other on whether the adverse effect can be avoided by changing the Descriptions of Entrustment or any other measures. However, if Data Exporter determines there is no such measure or the objective for which Data Exporter executed this Agreement will not be achieved by such measures, Data Exporter may terminate this Agreement with [   ] day prior written notice to Data Importer.

ARTICLE 9.   FEES AND PAYMENTS

As consideration for the entrustment hereunder, Data Exporter shall pay Data Importer the fee(s) set forth in

Exhibit C attached hereto in accordance with Exhibit C.

ARTICLE 10. TERM OF AGREEMENT

This Agreement shall come into force on the Effective Date, and, unless sooner terminated, shall continue in full force and effect for one (1) year from the Effective Date. Thereafter, this Agreement shall be automatically extended for successive periods of one (1) year each, unless either Party shall have otherwise notified to the other Party in writing at least [   ] prior to the expiry of this Agreement or any extension thereof.

ARTICLE 11.   TERMINATION

1. If Data Importer fails to comply with any provision of this Agreement and the failure has not been cured within [   ] after the receipt of a written notice from Data Exporter, Data Exporter may terminate this Agreement immediately by giving a written notice to Data Importer.
2. If Data Importer files a petition in bankruptcy or a petition in bankruptcy is filed against it, or if it becomes insolvent or bankrupt, makes a general assignment for the benefit of creditors, or goes into liquidation or receivership, Data Exporter may terminate this Agreement immediately by giving a written notice to Data Importer.
3. Data Exporter may terminate this Agreement at any time without cause by giving at least [   ] prior written notice to Data Importer.

ARTICLE 12.   EFFECTS OF TERMINATION OR EXPIRATION

1. Upon termination or expiration of this Agreement, Data Importer shall immediately (a) discontinue any handling of any Personal Data and (b) return or delete all the Personal Data according to Data Exporter's instruction, and (c) provide Data Exporter with a writing that an authorized representative of Data Importer certifies all the Personal Data were returned or destroyed. Data Exporter shall have the right, at its own expense, on

reasonable prior written notice, to inspect any record or information or facility to verify that all the Personal Data were returned or destroyed, or to have a third party conduct such inspection. Such inspection shall be conducted during reasonable business hours at the location where such record or information or the Personal Data may be stored.
2. The termination or expiration of this Agreement at any time, in any circumstances and for whatever reason does not exempt Data Importer from the obligations and/or conditions under this Agreement as regards the handling of the Personal Data provided to Data Importer.
3. In addition to paragraph 2 above, those provisions that by their nature should survive termination or expiration of this Agreement, will survive termination or expiration of this Agreement.

ARTICLE 13.   MISCELLANEOUS

1. This Agreement (including exhibits constituting a part of this Agreement) constitutes the entire agreement between the Parties with respect to the subject matter hereof and supersedes all prior agreements, understandings and negotiations, both written and oral, between the Parties with respect to the subject matter hereof. No modification of this Agreement shall be binding unless executed in writing by both Parties.
2. This Agreement may not be assigned or transferred by either Party without the express prior written consent of the other Party.
3. The waiver by each Party of a breach of any provision contained herein shall be in writing and shall in no way be construed as a waiver of any subsequent breach of such provision or the waiver of the provision itself.
4. Except as otherwise expressly provided in this Agreement, nothing contained in this Agreement shall be construed as creating a partnership, joint venture or agency relationship between the Parties or as granting either Party the authority to bind or contract in the name of or on the account of the other Party or to make any

statements, representations, warranties or commitments on behalf of the other Party.
5. If any provision of this Agreement shall be invalid or unenforceable, such invalidity or unenforceability shall not render the entire Agreement invalid. Rather, this Agreement shall be construed as if not containing the particular invalid or unenforceable provision, and the rights and obligations of each Party shall be construed and enforced accordingly.
6. Any notice, consent or other communication required or permitted to be given in writing hereunder (collectively "Notice") shall be (a) mailed by registered or certified mail, postage prepaid with return receipt requested, (b) sent by internationally recognized courier service (such as FedEx or DHL) which provides a delivery receipt, (c) delivered in person, or (d) sent by facsimile or electronic mail (with the sender's confirmation letter thereof sent by the registered or certified mail or the courier service), to the address specified below or to such changed address as may be specified by a like Notice from one Party to the other Party. If the Notice is mailed by registered or certified mail or sent by courier service, it shall be deemed to have been given [   ] business days after the mailing or sending. If the Notice is delivered in person or sent by facsimile or electronic mail, it shall be deemed to have been given upon receipt.

    If to Data Exporter:
        Name: [   ]
        Address: [   ]
        Attention: [   ]
        Facsimile number: [   ]
        Electronic mail address: [   ]

    If to Data Importer:
        Name: [   ]
        Address: [   ]
        Attention: [   ]
        Facsimile number: [   ]
        Electronic mail address: [   ]

7. This Agreement shall be construed in accordance with and governed by the laws of Japan without reference to principles of conflict of laws.
8. Any dispute arising out of or in connection with this Agreement, including any question regarding its existence, validity or termination, shall be referred to and finally resolved by arbitration administered by [   ] in accordance with [   ]. The seat of the arbitration shall be [   ]. The language of the arbitration shall be English.

IN WITNESS WHEREOF, the Parties have caused this Agreement to be executed by their duly authorized representatives as of the Effective Date.

Data Exporter

Company Name: [   ]

By: [   ]

Printed Name: [   ]

Title: [   ]

Data Importer

Company Name: [   ]

By: [   ]

Printed Name: [   ]

Title: [   ]

EXHIBIT A

Descriptions of the Personal Data
[   ]

Purpose of Entrustment
(Specify it as specific as possible)
[   ]

Descriptions of Entrustment
[Specify how to handle the Personal Data:
]

EXHIBIT B
SECURE MANAGEMENT MEASURES

[Examples]
Specify:
- If Data Importer has a certification for compliance with relevant ISO standards etc., such standards;
- If Data Exporter has made the secure management measures to be complied with by Data Importer, such measures;
- If Data Exporter finds Data Importer's own secure management measures is appropriate, such measures; or
- PPC's recommendations on security measures in the General GL or excerpt from the recommendations.

EXHIBIT C
FEES OF THE ENTRUSTMENT AND PAYMENTS

Index

Act on Specified Commercial Transactions, 70
Advertisements by E-mails, 74
AGREEMENT FOR ENTRUSTMENT OF HANDLING OF PERSONAL DATA, 98
Anonymously Processed Information, 5, 64
API, 5, 64
API GL, 5, 18
API Report, 5, 18
APPI, 5
ASCT, 70
big data, 16
Business operator, 5
Business Operator Handling Personal Information, 5, 22
CBPR, 54
Certification Mechanism, 53
Cloud Services, 36, 57
Codes of Conduct, 53
Collection in Relation to the Offering of Goods or Services, 25
Confirmation and Record GL, 5, 18
controller, 21, 22
Cookies, 75
Cross-Border Privacy Rules, 54
Data exporter, 6
Data importer, 6
Data Leakage, 7, 50
Data Protection Impact Assessment, 52
Data Protection Officer, 52
Data Subject's Consent, 29

Definitions of Basic Concepts, 19
DPIA, 52
DPO, 52
Entrustment of the Handling of Personal Data to a Third Party, 32
Extraterritorial Application, 25
Foreign GL, 6
GDPR, 6
general exceptional cases, 6, 26, 27, 28, 29, 34, 36
General GL, 6
Guidelines, 17
Handling etc. of Personal Data, 22
individual identification codes, 6, 19
Individual Number, 7, 25, 70
Information Disclosure to the Data Subject, 39
Japan EU Negotiation Toward Mutual Adequacy Findings, 62
Meibo-ya, 33
Monitoring of Data Subjects, 26
News Media etc., 24
Number Act, 7, 24, 70
Opt-out Mechanism, 7, 30
Order, 7, 17
Personal Data, 8, 20
PERSONAL DATA PROVISION AGREEMENT, 57, 77
Personal Information, 8, 19
Personal information database etc., 8, 20

Personal Information
  Protection Commission,
  Japan, 8, 62
Personal Information Requiring
  Special Consideration, 8, 22
PPC, 8, 62
Principles Relating to Handling
  of Personal Data, 26
Privacy Mark, 54
processing, 23
processor, 23
Providing or Receiving
  Personal Data, 29
Provision of Personal Data to a
  Third Party in a Foreign
  Country, 56
Provision to a Third Party, 29
Public Institutions, 8, 24
Q&A, 8, 19
Record Obligations, 33
Record the Handling of
  Personal Data, 47
Remedies, Liability, and
  Penalties, 63
Representative in Japan, 47
Retained Personal Data, 9, 21
Rights of the Data Subject, 42
Rules, 9, 17
Security of Handling, 48, 73
Specific Personal Information,
  9, 25, 70
Specification and Restriction of
  Purpose of Use (Purpose
  Limitation), 28
Statistical Information, 70
Supervision of Employees or a
  Third Party, 48
Supervisory Authority, 62
Transparency, 39
utilization of personal data, 16,
  17, 64

About the Author

Toshio Asai, Director of UniLaw Business Law Institute, which is engaged in research of business law issues.

He graduated from the Faculty of Law, Tohoku University in 1978, passed the 1998 examination of the patent attorney, and obtained a Certificate of American Law Study at Temple University Law School (Tokyo) in 2003. Since graduated from the University and until August 2017, he had been engaged in corporate legal affairs as a member or General Counsel of the legal departments of Japanese companies and foreign-affiliated companies. He is a member of the International Association of Privacy Professionals (IAPP), the Japanese Association of International Business Law, and GBL (Global Business Law) Institute. He has written articles and books listed in the "Authors' Articles and Books" in the next page, which are all in Japanese.

JAPAN DATA PROTECTION LAW
A Practical Guide in Comparison With GDPR
Issued in May 2018
Author: Toshio Asai

Authors' Articles and Books

- "Personal Information Protection Laws of Japan, US, EU and China and How to Comply With EU GDPR" Kindle book, March 2018
- "China Cybersecurity Law - Data Localization and Protection of Personal Information" Kindle book, October 2017
- " International Transfer of Personal Data - Comparison of Personal Data Protection Laws of Japan and EU and Their Application to Cloud Services " IBL (International Business Law), Vol. 45 No.10, October 2017, p.1462-1467
- "Practices of International Transfer of Personal Data Under Japan and EU Laws – Comparison Between Amended Act on Protection of Personal Information of Japan and EU GDPR" Kindle book, September 2017
- "Outline of US Defend Trade Secrets Act of 2016" Patent, December 2016
  https://system.jpaa.or.jp/patents_files_old/201612/jpaapatent201612_098-107.pdf
- "Royalty-Related Provisions and Royalty Audits" IBL (International Business Law), Vol. 44 No.11, November 2016, p.1720-1727
- "Global Business Law Basic - Training [2]: Intellectual Properties" Lexis Nexis Japan, October 2016
  Part 1, Chapter 2: Technology licensing business and the law
  Part 1, Chapter 3: Trademark licensing business and the law
  Part 2, Chapter 2: Intellectual property rights and parallel imports
  Appendixes: Samples of an international technology license agreement and international trademark license agreement
- "Trademark License and the Law" IBL (International Business Law), Vol. 44 No.10, October 2016, p.1563-1571
- "Finally Enacted!   US Defend Trade Secrets Act of 2016" BIZLAW, Lexis Nexis Japan, September 2016

- http://www.bizlaw.jp/blj_asai_01_01/
- "Technology License and the Law (3)" IBL (International Business Law). Vol. 44 No.9, September 2016, p.1421-1427
- "Technology License and the Law (2)" IBL (International Business Law), Vol. 44 No.8, August 2016, p.1264-1270
- "Technology License and the Law (1)" IBL (International Business Law), Vol. 44 No.7, July 2016, p.1102-1111
- "Trademark License Agreement in English" Patent, May 2014, p. 89-107
  https://system.jpaa.or.jp/patents_files_old/201404/jpaapatent201404_089-107.pdf
- "International Protection of Inventions" Patent, March 2014, p. 71-82
  https://system.jpaa.or.jp/patents_files_old/201403/jpaapatent201403_071-082.pdf
- "Patent License Agreement in English", Patent, February 2014, p. 66-85
  https://system.jpaa.or.jp/patents_files_old/201402/jpaapatent201402_066-085.pdf
- "International Protection of Trademarks" Patent, December 2013, p. 56-67
  https://system.jpaa.or.jp/patents_files_old/201310/jpaapatent201310_056-067.pdf
- "Non-Disclosure Agreement in English" Patent, May 2013, p.100-112 of the
  https://system.jpaa.or.jp/patents_files_old/201305/jpaapatent201305_100-112.pdf
- "Sample Clauses of Trademark License Agreement and the Points of Consideration" Business Law Journal, May 2013, p.76-88
- "From the First-to-Invent System to the First-to-File System – Outline of 2011 Amendment to US Patent Act" Business Law Journal, July 2012, p.108-115
- "Intellectual Property Rights and Parallel Import (2)" IBL (International Business Law), Vol. 39 No.11, November 2011, p.1680-1683
- "Intellectual Property Rights and Parallel Import (1)" IBL (International Business Law), Vol. 39 No.10, October 2011, p.1519-1523

- "Trademark and Patent Rights and Parallel Import" Business Law Journal, January 2011, p.112-116
- "Parallel Import of Copyrightable Works Into Japan and Its Legal Issues" Business Law Journal, July 2010, p.108-112
- "Anticounterfeiting Measures Against Counterfeits of Imported Brand Goods" Patent, March 2005, p. 64-67 https://system.jpaa.or.jp/patents_files_old/200503/jpaapatent200503_064-067.pdf
- "Relation Between IP Right Law and Antimonopoly Law - Contemporary Aspects of Competition Law (2)" Shinzansha, February 2005, p.885-902
- "The Drafting of Trademark License Agreement" Patent, February 2004, p. 37-56 https://system.jpaa.or.jp/patents_files_old/200402/jpaapatent200402_037-056.pdf
- "Considerations on the Drafting of a Patent License Clauses" Patent, July 2002, p.13-21 https://system.jpaa.or.jp/patents_files_old/200207/jpaapatent200207_013-021.pdf
- "Digitalization, Networking and the Protection of Graphic Works - a Map Database as an Example" Digitalization, Networking and Copyrights – 2001 Copyright Special Lectures Sponsored by Japanese Society for Rights of Authors (JASRAC), Seikei University, August 2002, p.156-163
- "Computer Network and Legal Department" NBL, No. 586, February 1996, p.3

www.ingramcontent.com/pod-product-compliance
Lightning Source LLC
Chambersburg PA
CBHW052327220526
45472CB00001B/300